DAILY LITURGY DEVOTIONAL

DAILY
LITURGY
DEVOTIONAL

40 Days of Worship
and Prayer

DOUGLAS SEAN
O'DONNELL

WHEATON, ILLINOIS

Daily Liturgy Devotional: 40 Days of Worship and Prayer

© 2024 by Crossway

Published by Crossway
   1300 Crescent Street
   Wheaton, Illinois 60187

Special thanks to Banner of Truth for permission to use and adapt material from Arthur Bennett, ed., *The Valley of Vision: A Collection of Puritan Prayers and Devotions* (1975; repr., Edinburgh: Banner of Truth Trust, 2006).

Special thanks to Philip Graham Ryken for permission to use and adapt material from *Luke: Knowing For Sure, Volume 1: Chapters 1–12*, Reformed Expository Commentary (Phillipsburg, NJ: P&R, 2009).

Special thanks to Barbara Duguid for permission to use and adapt select prayers from Barbara R. Duguid, *Streams of Mercy: Prayers of Confession and Celebration*, ed. Iain M. Duguid (Phillipsburg, NJ: P&R, 2018); *Prone to Wander: Prayers of Confession and Celebration*, ed. Iain M. Duguid (Phillipsburg, NJ: P&R, 2014).

Special thanks to Faith Alive Christian Resources for permission to use and adapt select prayers from Emily Blick and John D. Witvliet, eds., *Worship Sourcebook*, 2nd ed. (Grand Rapids, MI: Baker, 2013).

Special thanks to P&R for permission to use and adapt material from Douglas Sean O'Donnell, *God's Lyrics: Rediscovering Worship through Old Testament Songs* (Phillipsburg, NJ: P&R, 2010); *1–3 John: A Gospel-Transformed Life*, Reformed Expository Commentary (Phillipsburg, NJ: P&R, 2015); *Job: Where Wisdom Is Found*, Reformed Expository Commentary (Phillipsburg, NJ: P&R, forthcoming).

Cover design: Jordan Singer

First printing 2024

Printed in China

Hardcover ISBN: 978-1-4335-9578-3
ePub ISBN: 978-1-4335-9677-3
PDF ISBN: 978-1-4335-9676-6

Library of Congress Control Number: 2024936230

Crossway is a publishing ministry of Good News Publishers.

RRD			32	31	30	29	28	27	26	25	24
13	12	11	10	9	8	7	6	5	4	3	2	1

To my parents,
Winifred and Patrick O'Donnell,
with love and appreciation for teaching me to pray.

Christt with me,
Christ before me,
Christ behind me,
Christ in me,
Christ beneath me,
Christ above me.

FROM "ST. PATRICK'S BREASTPLATE"

Contents

Introduction xiii

THE GOSPEL

DAY 1 1

DAY 2 7

DAY 3 13

DAY 4 19

DAY 5 25

FAITH

DAY 6 31

DAY 7 37

DAY 8 43

DAY 9 49

DAY 10 55

LOVE

DAY 11 61

DAY 12 67

DAY 13 73

DAY 14 79

DAY 15 85

HOPE

DAY 16 91

DAY 17 97

DAY 18 103

DAY 19 109

DAY 20 115

WISDOM

DAY 21 121

DAY 22 127

DAY 23 133

DAY 24 139

DAY 25 145

HOLINESS

DAY 26 151

DAY 27 157

DAY 28 163

DAY 29 171

DAY 30 177

PERSEVERANCE

DAY 31 185

DAY 32 191

DAY 33 197

DAY 34 203

DAY 35 211

WITNESS

DAY 36 217

DAY 37 223

DAY 38 229

DAY 39 235

DAY 40 241

Notes 249

For Further Reading 253

Introduction to the

Daily Liturgy Devotional

40 Days of Worship and Prayer

One day, after Jesus finished praying, a disciple asked him, "Lord, teach us to pray" (Luke 11:1). Jesus responded with the Lord's Prayer (or the Disciples' Prayer!), a short and simple prayer that offers the perfect substance of and model for Christian prayer. The *Daily Liturgy Devotional*—with its prayers and patterns, Scriptures and songs—is designed to offer further help. If you struggle to pray, read God's word, or meditate upon what you have read, then this devotional will guide you; if you already practice good devotional habits, then this can serve as an additional resource to support you. The Greek word *leitourgia*, from which we get the word *liturgy*, is found a few times in the New Testament and can be translated as "service," "ministry," or "worship." So think of this *Daily Liturgy Devotional*, with its various set prayers and forms, not as boring or mechanical but as exciting and life-giving, a book that will *serve* you so that you might better *worship* God and *minister* to others.

The plan of this devotional is straightforward. For forty days you will reflect on eight themes, with each theme covering five days. Each theme is explored and reinforced in various ways each day: a Scripture reading, concise commentary on the passage, a memory verse, a classic hymn, and space for you to journal or write out personal prayers. Through these biblical and ancient Christian prayers you can offer your adoration and gratitude to God, confess your sins, and ask for help to read God's word and live the Christian life. If it helps, pray aloud and with physical gestures, such as raising your hands (1 Tim. 2:8) when you praise God's holy name or kneeling (Dan. 6:10) or lying prostrate (Luke 5:8) when you confess your sins. Using different postures to pray can engage your body and mind in new ways! "Stand up and bless the LORD your God from everlasting to everlasting" (Neh. 9:5). The devotional will remind you throughout of the important relationship between physical posture and spiritual disciplines.

The start of each day will follow a similar pattern. On the first day of the topic three traditional Christian prayers will lead you as you pray: the *Gloria Patri* (Latin for "Glory be to the Father"), the *Agnus Dei* (Latin for "Lamb of God"), and the Lord's Prayer (*Pater Noster* in Latin, if you are curious!). Then, for the other four days, the structure will follow the traditional pattern of adoration, confession, thanksgiving, and supplication, with each day featuring different prayers from the Old Testament and New Testament, along with old and new prayers. Prayers have all been adapted and edited for consistency of use within this volume, and I have included a page in the back that points to helpful primary and seconday resources, for those who would like to read more.

The *Daily Liturgy Devotional* allows for flexibility if you want to use the devotional for forty days straight or if you prefer to move at a slower pace. It is also designed to be your prayer guide for life, if desired. Use it over and over, day after day and year after year. Whether you use it for forty days or for forty years, I hope that much of the rich content—especially the memory verses, ancient prayers, and classic hymns—will be learned by heart and carried deep within your heart.

This book is dedicated to my mom (Winifred, or Winnie) and dad (Padraic, or Patrick), with love and appreciation for teaching me to pray. I specifically want to thank them for *taking me* to church each Sunday, where I learned to pray; enrolling me in school, where I learned many classic prayers of the church; and praying with me and my siblings at home (Padraic, Matthew, Julie, and Mary) before meals and bed. I fondly remember kneeling around a bed, holding hands, and together praying prayers such as the Lord's Prayer and the Gloria Patri. Thank you for that solid foundation! I am eternally grateful.

I would also like to thank the wonderful team I work with at Crossway, notably Don Jones, Erika Allen, Elliott Pinegar, Davis Wetherell, Josh McQuaid, Amy Warren, Leah Jolly, Jared Hughes, Jordan Singer, and Gerard Cruz. Thank you for your prayers, encouragements, and labors—designing, editing, typesetting, proofreading—for this project.

DOUGLAS SEAN O'DONNELL
Advent 2023

The Gospel

Part 1 of 5

Through these biblical and ancient Christian prayers offer your adoration and gratitude to God, confess your sins, and ask for help to read his word and live the Christian life. If it helps, pray aloud and with physical gestures, such as raising your hands (1 Tim. 2:8) when you praise God's holy name or kneeling (Dan. 6:10) or lying prostrate (Luke 5:8) when you confess your sins. Using different postures to pray can engage your body and mind in new ways! "Stand up and bless the Lord your God from everlasting to everlasting" (Neh. 9:5).

Gloria Patri
Pray the Gloria Patri. Then take time to praise and thank God for specific blessings in your life.

Glory be to the Father, and to the Son, and to the Holy Ghost,
As it was in the beginning, is now, and ever shall be,
    world without end.
Amen.

Agnus Dei
Pray the Agnus Dei. Then take time to ask God through Jesus to forgive specific sins. Also offer prayers of lament. Pray that God would deal with sufferings and injustices both now and when Christ returns. Cry out, "O Sovereign

Lord, holy and true, how long before you will judge and avenge our blood on those who dwell on the earth?" (Rev. 6:10), or "Out of the depths I cry to you, O LORD! O Lord, hear my voice! Let your ears be attentive to the voice of my pleas for mercy!" (Ps. 130:1–2).

Lamb of God, who takes away the sins of the world,
    have mercy on us.
Lamb of God, who takes away the sins of the world,
    have mercy on us.
Lamb of God, who takes away the sins of the world,
    grant us peace. Amen.

The Lord's Prayer
Pray each line slowly. As you think about each petition, add your own specific requests.

Our Father in heaven,
hallowed be your name.
Your kingdom come,
your will be done,
    on earth as it is in heaven.
Give us this day our daily bread,
and forgive us our debts,
    as we also have forgiven our debtors.
And lead us not into temptation,
    but deliver us from evil.   Matthew 6:9–13

Prayer of Illumination
Ask God's Spirit to bring to light the meaning and application of God's word.

Thus says the LORD:
"Heaven is my throne,
    and the earth is my footstool;

what is the house that you would build for me,
and what is the place of my rest?
All these things my hand has made,
and so all these things came to be,
declares the LORD.
But this is the one to whom I will look:
he who is humble and contrite in spirit
and trembles at my word." *Isaiah 66:1–2*

Lord, as I now commit to reading and learning from your word with the desire to live under your authority and to build my life on your truth, I ask that you would give me a humble and contrite spirit that trembles at your word. Amen.

• • •

Scripture Reading

Paul, a servant of Christ Jesus, called to be an apostle, set apart for the gospel of God, which he promised beforehand through his prophets in the holy Scriptures, concerning his Son, who was descended from David according to the flesh and was declared to be the Son of God in power according to the Spirit of holiness by his resurrection from the dead, Jesus Christ our Lord, through whom we have received grace and apostleship to bring about the obedience of faith for the sake of his name among all the nations, including you who are called to belong to Jesus Christ,

To all those in Rome who are loved by God and called to be saints:

Grace to you and peace from God our Father and the Lord Jesus Christ. *Romans 1:1–7*

Concise Commentary

Our memory verse for the first five days is 1 Corinthians 15:3–4, where Paul writes about the gospel that he preached, stating,

"I delivered to you as of first importance what I also received: that Christ died for our sins in accordance with the Scriptures, that he was buried, that he was raised on the third day in accordance with the Scriptures." If the gospel is of first importance, then we should know it! So, if someone asked, "What is the gospel?" what would we say? We might be accustomed to focusing on (1) *who Jesus is* (the Son of God whom the Father sent into the world), (2) *what Jesus did* (he lived, died, and rose again), and (3) *what we receive* if we believe in Jesus (the forgiveness of sins and eternal life). And indeed, when Paul writes about the gospel in Romans 1, he mentions these three things: *who Jesus is* ("the Son of God" and "our Lord"), *what he has done* ("resurrection from the dead"), and *what we receive* if we believe ("salvation," Rom. 1:16). But he also adds two other components. First, he says that God's gospel was "promised beforehand through his prophets in the holy Scriptures" (1:2). It is good news, but it is not new news! Second, he writes of the recipients of the gospel, namely, people from "all the nations" (1:5)—that is, "*everyone who believes*" (1:16). So, no matter what tongue, tribe, or people you are from, you can come to Jesus, recognize your need for him, call out in faith for the forgiveness of your sins, and receive God's mercy.

Prayer Prompt

Take time today to thank God the Father that the good news about Jesus's life, death, and resurrection is for you and, by God's grace, has come to you and has spread to all nations. Pray for help to hold fast to the word you have received. Ask the Holy Spirit to bring to mind people you know who need to come to Jesus, to recognize their need for him, to call out in faith for forgiveness, and to receive God's mercy. Pray for them and pray for the courage to bear witness to them about who Christ is and what he has done.

Memory Verse

For I delivered to you as of first importance what I also received: that Christ died for our sins in accordance with the Scriptures, that he was buried, that he was raised on the third day in accordance with the Scriptures.

1 Corinthians 15:3–4

• • •

"When I Survey the Wondrous Cross"
Isaac Watts • *1707*

When I survey the wondrous cross
on which the Prince of glory died,
my richest gain I count but loss,
and pour contempt on all my pride.

Forbid it, Lord, that I should boast
save in the death of Christ, my God!
All the vain things that charm me most,
I sacrifice them to his blood.

See, from his head, his hands, his feet,
sorrow and love flow mingled down.
Did e'er such love and sorrow meet,
or thorns compose so rich a crown?

Were the whole realm of nature mine,
that were a present far too small.
Love so amazing, so divine,
demands my soul, my life, my all.

The Gospel

Part 2 of 5

Adoration
Pray the prayer below. Then pause to praise God for who he is and what he has done.

I confess that great indeed is the mystery of godliness (revealed in Jesus!)—that "he was manifested in the flesh, vindicated by the Spirit, seen by angels, proclaimed among the nations, believed on in the world, taken up in glory" (1 Tim. 3:16). I praise you, Lord Jesus, for your life, death, resurrection, and ascension and that the gospel has been—and continues to be—proclaimed throughout the world. Amen.

Confession
Pray the prayer below. Then take time to ask God through Jesus to forgive specific sins.

O Lord, you who are all merciful, take away my sins from me and kindle within me the fire of your Holy Spirit. Take away my heart of stone and give me a heart of flesh and blood, a heart to love and adore you, a heart to delight in you, a heart that always desires to please you and live for you, for the sake of Christ's glory. Amen.   *Ambrose*

Thanksgiving

Thank God for the truth that "If we confess our sins, he is faithful and just to forgive us our sins and to cleanse us from all unrighteousness" (1 John 1:9), then pray the prayer below. Finally, take time to thank God for specific blessings in your life. Also feel free to offer Psalm 118:1 ("Oh give thanks to the LORD, for he is good; for his steadfast love endures forever!") as a repeated refrain as you list off (and lift up!) to God people, events, gifts, and circumstances for which you are thankful.

Oh come, let us sing to the LORD;
> let us make a joyful noise to the rock of our salvation!
Let us come into his presence with thanksgiving;
> let us make a joyful noise to him with songs of praise!
> Psalm 95:1–2

Supplication

After you pray the prayer below, feel free to add your own specific requests.

Lord, help me walk in a manner worthy of the gospel. So, help me not to be self-willing or self-glorying, a drunkard, argumentative, fond of sordid gain or a lover of money, but to be above reproach, faithful in my relationships, hospitable (giving time, thought, and prayer to those in need within my church and community), loving of what is good, sensible, just, devout, self-controlled, steadfast in the truth of the gospel. Amen. *Based on 1 Timothy 3:3–7; Titus 1:6–9*

Prayer of Illumination

Almighty God and most merciful Father, I humbly submit myself to you and fall down before your Majesty, asking you from the bottom of my heart that this seed of your word that I am about to read may take such deep root that neither the burning heat of persecution cause it to wither, nor the thorny cares of this life choke it. But that, as seed sown in good ground, it may bring forth thirty, sixty, or even a hundredfold, as your heavenly wisdom has appointed it. Amen.   *Middleburg Liturgy (1586)*

◆ ◆ ◆

Scripture Reading

As for the word that he sent to Israel, preaching good news of peace through Jesus Christ (he is Lord of all), you yourselves know what happened throughout all Judea, beginning from Galilee after the baptism that John proclaimed: how God anointed Jesus of Nazareth with the Holy Spirit and with power. He went about doing good and healing all who were oppressed by the devil, for God was with him. And we are witnesses of all that he did both in the country of the Jews and in Jerusalem. They put him to death by hanging him on a tree, but God raised him on the third day and made him to appear, not to all the people but to us who had been chosen by God as witnesses, who ate and drank with him after he rose from the dead. And he commanded us to preach to the people and to testify that he is the one appointed by God to be judge of the living and the dead. To him all the prophets bear witness that everyone who believes in him receives forgiveness of sins through his name.   *Acts 10:36–43*

Concise Commentary

The gospel message outlined in Peter's sermon includes the lordship of Jesus; the ministry of John the Baptist; the life of Jesus in Galilee; Jesus's power, miracles, healings, and exorcisms; the death of Jesus by crucifixion; his resurrection; his appearances to the believers in full bodily form after his death; the command to preach forgiveness of sins through faith in Christ; and the assertion that the Old Testament prophecies pointed to all these things. What is interesting is that Peter's outline exemplifies the essence of the gospel as preached throughout Acts: God's offer of salvation; the life, death, and resurrection of Jesus; and the call to faith in light of coming judgment (see Acts 2:14–36; 3:17–26; 4:8–12; 5:29–32; 7:2–53; 10:34–43; 13:16–41; 17:22–31; 20:18–35; 22:1–21; 24:10–21; 26:2–23; 28:25–28). Moreover, his outline surely reflects the outline of the four Gospels, most notably of Mark.

Acts 10	Mark
"good news" (10:36)	"the beginning of the gospel" (1:1)
"God anointed Jesus of Nazareth with the Holy Spirit" (10:38)	The coming of the Spirit on Jesus (1:10)
"beginning from Galilee" (10:37)	The Galilean ministry (1:16—8:26)
"He went about doing good and healing all who were oppressed by the devil" (10:38)	Jesus's ministry focuses on healings and exorcisms (e.g., 1:32–34)
"we are witnesses of all that he did . . . in Jerusalem" (10:39)	Ministry in Jerusalem (Mark 11–14)
"They put him to death by hanging him on a tree" (10:39)	Focus on the death of Christ (Mark 15)
"God raised him on the third day" (10:40)	The resurrection (Mark 16): "He has risen; he is not here." (16:6)

Prayer Prompt

Take time today to thank God that he has provided clear passages in his word to teach us the gospel. Also thank the Father, Son, and Spirit for giving you faith. Ask for God's help both to live out faithfully and to share God's offer of salvation. Pray specifically (feel free to write out names) for family, friends, and coworkers who need to hear the good news that, in Jesus, God is making all things new. Pray for prayerfulness (that you would pray for them often!) and courage (that you would regularly bear witness—in word and deed).

Memory Verse

For I delivered to you as of first importance what I also received: that Christ died for our sins in accordance with the Scriptures, that he was buried, that he was raised on the third day in accordance with the Scriptures. *1 Corinthians 15:3–4*

❖ ❖ ❖

"O Sacred Head, Now Wounded"
Attributed to Bernard of Clairvaux | trans. James W. Alexander • 1829

O sacred Head, now wounded,
with grief and shame weighed down,
now scornfully surrounded
with thorns, Thine only crown.
O sacred Head, what glory,
what bliss till now was Thine!
Yet, though despised and gory,
I joy to call Thee mine.

What Thou, my Lord, hast suffered
was all for sinners' gain;
mine, mine was the transgression,
but Thine the deadly pain.
Lo, here I fall, my Savior!
'Tis I deserve Thy place;
look on me with Thy favor,
vouchsafe to me Thy grace.

What language shall I borrow
to thank Thee, dearest Friend,

for this, Thy dying sorrow,
Thy pity without end?
O make me Thine forever!
And should I fainting be,
Lord, let me never, never
outlive my love for Thee.

3

The Gospel

Part 3 of 5

Adoration
Pray the prayer below. Then pause to praise God for who he is and for what he has done.

Praise God from whom all blessings flow;
Praise him all creatures here below;
Praise him above ye heav'nly host;
Praise Father, Son, and Holy Ghost. Amen.

Confession
Pray the prayer below. Then take time to ask God through Jesus to forgive specific sins.

Merciful Father, I have strayed from your ways like a lost sheep. I have followed too much the schemes and desires of my own heart and have broken your holy laws. I have left undone what I ought to have done, and I have done what I ought not to have done. Yet, good Lord, have mercy on me. I repent! Restore me now according to the promises declared to me through your Son, Jesus Christ. And grant, merciful Father, for his sake, that from now on I may live a godly and obedient life, to the glory of your holy name. Amen.   *Book of Common Prayer (1662)*

Thanksgiving

Thank God for the truth that "If we confess our sins, he is faithful and just to forgive us our sins and to cleanse us from all unrighteousness" (1 John 1:9), then pray the prayer below. Finally, take time to thank God for specific blessings in your life. Also feel free to offer Psalm 118:1 ("Oh give thanks to the LORD, *for he is good; for his steadfast love endures forever!") as a repeated refrain as you list off (and lift up!) to God people, events, gifts, and circumstances for which you are thankful.*

Father, I thank you for the Lord Jesus Christ, the only mediator between God and man. I thank you for his perpetual cleansing blood, for your constant forgiveness through him. I thank you for the gospel—the good news of salvation through Christ. And I thank you for the work of the Holy Spirit in my heart, mind, and will to embrace this glorious message of salvation. Amen.

Supplication

After you pray the prayer below, feel free to add your own specific requests.

Keep back your servant also from presumptuous sins;
    let them not have dominion over me!
Then I shall be blameless,
    and innocent of great transgression.

Let the words of my mouth and the meditation of my heart
    be acceptable in your sight,
    O LORD, my rock and my redeemer.   Psalm 19:13–14

Prayer of Illumination

O make your word a swift word, passing from the ear to the heart, from the heart to the lip and conversation; that, as the rain returns not empty, so neither may your word, but accomplish that for which it is given. Amen.   *George Herbert*

• • •

Scripture Reading

He is the image of the invisible God, the firstborn of all creation. For by him all things were created, in heaven and on earth, visible and invisible, whether thrones or dominions or rulers or authorities—all things were created through him and for him. And he is before all things, and in him all things hold together. And he is the head of the body, the church. He is the beginning, the firstborn from the dead, that in everything he might be preeminent. For in him all the fullness of God was pleased to dwell, and through him to reconcile to himself all things, whether on earth or in heaven, making peace by the blood of his cross.

And you, who once were alienated and hostile in mind, doing evil deeds, he has now reconciled in his body of flesh by his death, in order to present you holy and blameless and above reproach before him, if indeed you continue in the faith, stable and steadfast, not shifting from the hope of the gospel that you heard, which has been proclaimed in all creation under heaven, and of which I, Paul, became a minister.   *Colossians 1:15–23*

Concise Commentary

This beautifully poetic passage can be divided nicely into two parts. The first part focuses on Christ; the second on Christians. The first part refers to Jesus with the pronouns "he," "his," "him," and "himself" thirteen times. We can label these verses *He Is*: "He is the image of the invisible God"; "he is before all things"; "he is the head of the body, the church"; and "he is the beginning, the firstborn from the dead." The second part still speaks about Jesus—what his death accomplishes—but the focus falls on the church's response to the person and work of Jesus. We can call these verses *And You*. Verse 21 begins, "And you, who once were alienated and hostile in mind"; verse 22 uses the phrase "to present you holy and blameless," and verse 23 says "if indeed you continue in the faith." Put these together—He Is and And You—and we see the point Paul is making: Jesus Christ, who is *supreme* over creation (1:15–17) and in the church, the new creation (1:18), is our *sufficient* Savior. Through his death Jesus has made "peace [with God] by the blood of his cross," and "he has now reconciled [you all] in his body of flesh by his death, in order to present you holy and blameless and above reproach before him" (1:22). What good news! God, through his supreme-over-creation and sufficient-for-salvation Son, "has delivered us from the domain of darkness and transferred us to the kingdom of his beloved Son" (1:13).

Prayer Prompt
Take time to "thank God, the Father" of our "Lord Jesus Christ" that you believe "the word of truth, the gospel." Beyond the gift of faith ("your faith in Christ Jesus"), thank him for the gifts of love (that "you have [love] for all the saints") and hope ("the hope laid up for you in heaven"). Ask God, as Paul prayed for the church, that "you may be filled with the knowledge of his will in all spiritual wisdom and understanding, so as to walk in a manner worthy of the Lord, fully pleasing to him: bearing fruit in every good work and increasing in the knowledge of God; being strengthened with all power, according to his glorious might, for all endurance and patience with joy." Pray that "as you received Christ Jesus as Lord, so [you would] walk in him." Based on Colossians 1:3–5, 9–11; 2:6

Memory Verse
For I delivered to you as of first importance what I also received: that Christ died for our sins in accordance with the Scriptures, that he was buried, that he was raised on the third day in accordance with the Scriptures. 1 Corinthians 15:3–4

. . .

"Fairest Lord Jesus"
trans. Joseph Seiss • 1873

Fairest Lord Jesus, Ruler of all nature,
O thou of God and man the Son;
thee will I cherish, thee will I honor,
thou, my soul's glory, joy, and crown.

Fair are the meadows, fairer still the woodlands,
robed in the blooming garb of spring:
Jesus is fairer, Jesus is purer,
who makes the woeful heart to sing.

Fair is the sunshine, fairer still the moonlight,
and all the twinkling, starry host:
Jesus shines brighter, Jesus shines purer,
than all the angels heaven can boast.

Beautiful Savior! Lord of all the nations!
Son of God and Son of Man!
Glory and honor, praise, adoration,
now and forevermore be thine.

4

The Gospel

Part 4 of 5

Adoration

Pray the prayer below. Then pause to praise God for who he is and for what he has done.

Great and amazing are your deeds,
  O Lord God the Almighty!
Just and true are your ways,
  O King of the nations!
Who will not fear, O Lord,
  and glorify your name?
For you alone are holy.
  All nations will come
  and worship you,
for your righteous acts have been revealed.   *Revelation 15:3–4*

Confession

Pray the prayer below. Then take time to ask God through Jesus to forgive specific sins.

O Lord, my great and awesome God, who keeps covenant and steadfast love with those who love you and keep your commandments, I acknowledge that I have sinned and done wrong and turned aside from your commandments. Forgive me, God of mercy, for all the times I have rebelled against you and have not obeyed your voice. God, please listen to my pleas for mercy, and for your own sake make your face to shine upon me. For I present my pleas before you not because of my righteousness but because of your great mercy. O Lord, hear; O Lord, forgive. Amen.   *Based on Daniel 9:3–18*

Thanksgiving

Thank God for the truth that "If we confess our sins, he is faithful and just to forgive us our sins and to cleanse us from all unrighteousness" (1 John 1:9), then pray the prayer below. Finally, take time to thank God for specific blessings in your life. Also feel free to offer Psalm 118:1 ("Oh give thanks to the Lord, *for he is good; for his steadfast love endures forever!") as a repeated refrain as you list off (and lift up!) to God people, events, gifts, and circumstances for which you are thankful.*

[Along with your church, I] give thanks to you, Lord God
     Almighty,
  who is and who was,
for you have taken your great power
  and begun to reign.
The nations raged,
  but your wrath came,
  and the time for the dead to be judged,
and for rewarding your servants, the prophets and saints,
  and those who fear your name,
  both small and great,
and for destroying the destroyers of the earth.   *Revelation 11:17–18*

Supplication

After you pray the prayer below, feel free to add your own specific requests.

God of all comfort, I pray for the brokenhearted, that you would mend them; for the sick, that you would heal them;

for the proud, that you would humble them; for the weak, that you would strengthen them; and for the apathetic, that you would enliven them. I also pray, Lord, that I would find my rest and comfort in you and, in turn, offer your rest and comfort to others—for their good and to the glory of your name. Amen.

Prayer of Illumination
Spirit of God, who breathed life into all creation, fill me afresh with your grace and wisdom and power as I read your breathed-out word. Amen.

• • •

Scripture Reading
Then I saw in the right hand of him who was seated on the throne a scroll written within and on the back, sealed with seven seals. And I saw a mighty angel proclaiming with a loud voice, "Who is worthy to open the scroll and break its seals?" And no one in heaven or on earth or under the earth was able to open the scroll or to look into it, and I began to weep loudly because no one was found worthy to open the scroll or to look into it. And one of the elders said to me, "Weep no more; behold, the Lion of the tribe of Judah, the Root of David, has conquered, so that he can open the scroll and its seven seals."

And between the throne and the four living creatures and among the elders I saw a Lamb standing, as though it had been slain, with seven horns and with seven eyes, which are the seven spirits of God sent out into all the earth. And he went and took the scroll from the right hand of him who was seated on the throne. And when he had taken the scroll, the four living creatures and the twenty-four elders fell down before the Lamb, each holding a harp, and golden bowls full of incense, which are the prayers of the saints. And they sang a new song, saying,

"Worthy are you to take the scroll
    and to open its seals,
for you were slain, and by your blood you ransomed people
        for God
    from every tribe and language and people and nation,
and you have made them a kingdom and priests to our God,
    and they shall reign on the earth."

Then I looked, and I heard around the throne and the living creatures and the elders the voice of many angels, numbering myriads of myriads and thousands of thousands, saying with a loud voice,

"Worthy is the Lamb who was slain,
to receive power and wealth and wisdom and might
and honor and glory and blessing!"

And I heard every creature in heaven and on earth and under the earth and in the sea, and all that is in them, saying,

"To him who sits on the throne and to the Lamb
be blessing and honor and glory and might forever and ever!"

And the four living creatures said, "Amen!" and the elders fell down and worshiped.   *Revelation 5:1–14*

Concise Commentary

The reason the Lamb is worthy to open the scroll is because he is the rightful king ("the Lion of the tribe of Judah" and "the root of David," 5:5) who has conquered through the cross. Four times throughout Revelation Jesus is depicted as a slain lamb (5:6; 7:14; 12:11; 13:8). This repetition shows that, for John, the cross is central to his proclamation of the gospel. Jesus's blood both ransoms people from all the nations ("by your blood you ransomed people for God from every tribe and language and people and nation," 5:9) and makes those who were once unworthy (see 5:3–4) now holy (into "a kingdom and priests to our God" who "shall reign on the earth," 5:10). The only proper response to the sacrifice of the Lion-Lamb is to worship him, to fall down before him and join the million-tongued chorus of heaven "saying with a loud voice, 'Worthy is the Lamb who was slain, to receive power and wealth and wisdom and might and honor and glory and blessing!'" (5:12).

Prayer Prompt
Take time to focus on Christ and him crucified. Thank God that through Jesus's sacrifice you have been ransomed from your sin, called into his eternal kingdom, and granted every heavenly blessing. Pray for his help to witness faithfully to the power and mercy of Christ today.

> Memory Verse
> For I delivered to you as of first importance what I also received: that Christ died for our sins in accordance with the Scriptures, that he was buried, that he was raised on the third day in accordance with the Scriptures.   *1 Corinthians 15:3–4*

* * *

"Nothing But the Blood of Jesus"
Robert Lowry · 1876

What can wash away my sin?
Nothing but the blood of Jesus.
What can make me whole again?
Nothing but the blood of Jesus.

O precious is the flow
that makes me white as snow;
no other fount I know;
nothing but the blood of Jesus.

For my pardon this I see:
nothing but the blood of Jesus.
For my cleansing this my plea:
nothing but the blood of Jesus.

REFRAIN

Nothing can for sin atone:
nothing but the blood of Jesus.
Naught of good that I have done:
nothing but the blood of Jesus.

REFRAIN

This is all my hope and peace:
nothing but the blood of Jesus.
This is all my righteousness:
nothing but the blood of Jesus.

REFRAIN

The Gospel

Part 5 of 5

Adoration

Pray the prayer below. Then pause to praise God for who he is and for what he has done.

Lord Jesus, after your resurrection from the grave and ascension into heaven God the Father highly exalted you and gave you a name that is above every name, so that at your return and the judgment every knee will bow in heaven (the knee of every angel and archangel and the saints above), and every knee will bow on earth (the knee of every believer and nonbeliever alike), and every knee will bow under the earth (the knee of every demon and Satan himself) and confess that "Jesus Christ is Lord, to the glory of God the Father." Today I confess (and rejoice!) that you are Jesus (the incarnate Son of God), that you are the Christ (the Messiah, the yes to every promise of God), and that you are the Lord, the God of both covenants. Amen.   *Based on Philippians 2:1–11*

Confession

Pray the prayer below. Then take time to ask God through Jesus to forgive specific sins.

Hide your face from my sins,
    and blot out all my iniquities.

Create in me a clean heart, O God,
 and renew a right spirit within me.   Psalm 51:9–10

Thanksgiving

Thank God for the truth that "If we confess our sins, he is faithful and just to forgive us our sins and to cleanse us from all unrighteousness" (1 John 1:9), then pray the prayer below. Finally, take time to thank God for specific blessings in your life. Also feel free to offer Psalm 118:1 ("Oh give thanks to the Lord, for he is good; for his steadfast love endures forever!") as a repeated refrain as you list off (and lift up!) to God people, events, gifts, and circumstances for which you are thankful.

O Lord, God Almighty, you are the creator and governor of the world. I thank you that, while we are born to trouble and you have appointed the grave to be the end of all living, you have not left us without hope in that world that is to come. Today I thank you for the gift of Jesus Christ your Son, by whose gospel life and immortality are brought to light. I thank you for the pardon of sin through faith in a redeemer; for the guidance of your providence; and for the consolations of your Spirit. I thank you for giving us weekly rest (the Sabbath); for your written word; and for all the other means of grace. Thank you! Amen.
Henry Thornton

Supplication

After you pray the prayer below, feel free to add your own specific requests.

Heavenly Father, I worship you as the creator and sustainer of the universe. Lord Jesus, I worship you, Savior and Lord of the world. Holy Spirit, I worship you, sanctifier of the people of God. Glory to the Father and to the Son and to the Holy Spirit. Heavenly Father, I pray that I may live this day in your presence and please you more and more. Lord Jesus, I pray that this day I may take up my cross and follow you. Holy Spirit, I pray that this day you will fill me with yourself and cause your fruit to ripen in my life: love, joy, peace, patience, kindness, goodness, faithfulness, gentleness, and self-control. Holy, blessed, and glorious Trinity, three persons in one God, have mercy upon me. Amen.   *John Stott*

Prayer of Illumination
Spirit of God, you have breathed life into your holy word. I ask that you would fill me afresh now with your presence and power so that I might rightly understand and apply your sacred truth to my life. Amen.

◆ ◆ ◆

Scripture Reading
And while he was at Bethany in the house of Simon the leper, as he was reclining at table, a woman came with an alabaster flask of ointment of pure nard, very costly, and she broke the flask and poured it over his head. There were some who said to themselves indignantly, "Why was the ointment wasted like that? For this ointment could have been sold for more than three hundred denarii and given to the poor." And they scolded her. But Jesus said, "Leave her alone. Why do you trouble her? She has done a beautiful thing to me. For you always have the poor with you, and whenever you want, you can do good for them. But you will not always have me. She has done what she could; she has anointed my body beforehand for burial. And truly, I say to you, wherever the gospel is proclaimed in the whole world, what she has done will be told in memory of her."   *Mark 14:3–9*

Concise Commentary
In the scene Mark sets between the Passover plot (Mark 14:1–2) and Judas's scheme to betray Jesus (14:10–11) he records a love story, one of the greatest love stories in the Greatest Love Story

ever told. It is a short story (told in one verse), but also a spectacular one: "And while he was at Bethany in the house of Simon the leper, as he was reclining at table, a woman came with an alabaster flask of ointment of pure nard, very costly, and she broke the flask and poured it over his head" (14:3). Mark's description of this woman's identity and motives is sparse. However, his description of what she did and how both the disciples and Jesus reacted is quite detailed. She came into the house, approached Jesus with a "very costly" perfume (made of "pure nard") contained in an ornate bottle ("an alabaster flask"), and then "broke" the seal and poured all the ointment over Jesus's head (14:3). Some of the men around the dinner table were so upset that "they scolded her" (14:5). But Jesus was well pleased. After he rebuked those who rebuked her ("Leave her alone. Why do you trouble her?") and labeled *beautiful* what they called *wasteful* (14:6), he announced this commendation/prophecy: "Truly, I say to you, wherever the gospel is proclaimed in the whole world, what she has done will be told in memory of her" (14:9). Whether the term "the gospel" refers to the Gospel of Mark (as it is read or recited aloud) or to the passion narrative, her sweet perfume that filled this leper's house now fills the four corners and seven continents of the world.[1]

Prayer Prompt

Take time to ask God, through his Spirit, to renew your love for Jesus—to help you acknowledge that Jesus deserves your highest outpouring of love. He deserves your strangely extravagant and shockingly costly love.

Memory Verse

For I delivered to you as of first importance what I also received: that Christ died for our sins in accordance with the Scriptures, that he was buried, that he was raised on the third day in accordance with the Scriptures.   *1 Corinthians 15:3–4*

* * *

"My Jesus, I Love Thee"
William Ralph Featherston • *1864*

My Jesus, I love Thee, I know Thou art mine;
For Thee all the follies of sin I resign.
My gracious Redeemer, my Savior art Thou;
If ever I loved Thee, my Jesus, 'tis now.

I love Thee because Thou has first lov-ed me,
And purchased my pardon on Calvary's tree.
I love Thee for wearing the thorns on Thy brow;
If ever I loved Thee, my Jesus, 'tis now.

I'll love Thee in life, I will love Thee in death,
And praise Thee as long as Thou lendest me breath;
And say when the death dew lies cold on my brow,
If ever I loved Thee, my Jesus, 'tis now.

In mansions of glory and endless delight,
I'll ever adore Thee in heaven so bright;
I'll sing with the glittering crown on my brow;
If ever I loved Thee, my Jesus, 'tis now.

6

Faith

Part 1 of 5

Through these biblical and ancient Christian prayers offer your adoration and gratitude to God, confess your sins, and ask for help to read his word and live the Christian life. If it helps, pray aloud and with physical gestures, such as raising your hands (1 Tim. 2:8) when you praise God's holy name or kneeling (Dan. 6:10) or lying prostrate (Luke 5:8) when you confess your sins. Using different postures to pray can engage your body and mind in new ways! "Stand up and bless the LORD your God from everlasting to everlasting" (Neh. 9:5).

Gloria Patri
Pray the Gloria Patri. Then take time to praise and thank God for specific blessings in your life.

Glory be to the Father, and to the Son, and to the Holy Ghost,
As it was in the beginning, is now, and ever shall be,
 world without end.
Amen.

Agnus Dei
Pray the Agnus Dei. Then take time to ask God through Jesus to forgive specific sins. Also offer prayers of lament. Pray that God would deal with sufferings and injustices both now and when Christ returns. Cry out, "O Sovereign

Lord, holy and true, how long before you will judge and avenge our blood on those who dwell on the earth?" (Rev. 6:10), or "Out of the depths I cry to you, O LORD! O Lord, hear my voice! Let your ears be attentive to the voice of my pleas for mercy!" (Ps. 130:1–2).

Lamb of God, who takes away the sins of the world,
    have mercy on us.
Lamb of God, who takes away the sins of the world,
    have mercy on us.
Lamb of God, who takes away the sins of the world,
    grant us peace. Amen.

The Lord's Prayer
Pray each line slowly. As you think about each petition, add your own specific requests.

Our Father in heaven,
hallowed be your name.
Your kingdom come,
your will be done,
    on earth as it is in heaven.
Give us this day our daily bread,
and forgive us our debts,
    as we also have forgiven our debtors.
And lead us not into temptation,
    but deliver us from evil.   *Matthew 6:9–13*

Prayer of Illumination
Spirit of God, I know that your inspired word is a lamp to my feet and a light to my path. Renew my mind to understand these words, soften my heart to love you, and strengthen my will to follow in your ways. Amen.

◆ ◆ ◆

Scripture Reading

Now faith is the assurance of things hoped for, the conviction of things not seen. For by it the people of old received their commendation. By faith we understand that the universe was created by the word of God, so that what is seen was not made out of things that are visible.

By faith Abel offered to God a more acceptable sacrifice than Cain, through which he was commended as righteous, God commending him by accepting his gifts. And through his faith, though he died, he still speaks. By faith Enoch was taken up so that he should not see death, and he was not found, because God had taken him. Now before he was taken he was commended as having pleased God. And without faith it is impossible to please him, for whoever would draw near to God must believe that he exists and that he rewards those who seek him. . . .

Therefore, since we are surrounded by so great a cloud of witnesses, let us also lay aside every weight, and sin which clings so closely, and let us run with endurance the race that is set before us, looking to Jesus, the founder and perfecter of our faith, who for the joy that was set before him endured the cross, despising the shame, and is seated at the right hand of the throne of God.
Hebrews 11:1–6; 12:1–2

Concise Commentary

There is only one definition of faith given in the Bible—the one here in Hebrews 11:1 ("Faith is . . ."). This does not mean that other verses and stories in Scripture do not help us understand the nature of biblical faith; the author of Hebrews proves as much when he lists sixteen examples of faith, characters who all have stories and key verses that can summarize their faith. For example, Abraham showed faith in God's resurrection power through his willingness to offer Isaac on the altar, and his faith, as exemplified throughout his life, is summarized in Genesis 15:6: Abraham "believed the LORD, and he counted it to him as righteousness." Paul builds his doctrine of justification by faith upon this verse and illustrates the nature of saving faith through the story of Abraham (see Rom. 4). Another example (one not referenced in Heb. 11–12) is Habakkuk. After the Lord reveals his purposes for Judah and Babylon, and after Habakkuk grasps that he must trust in the Lord even if he does not comprehend fully the Lord's providence, he offers a beautiful song of faith in Habakkuk 3 and also receives one of the most significant summaries of faith in Scripture: "The righteous shall live by his faith" (Hab. 2:4), quoted three times in the New Testament (Rom. 1:17; Gal. 3:11; Heb. 10:38, which is immediately before 11:1).

Notice in Hebrews 11:1 that, to the author, faith has a future focus, notably "Jesus, the founder and perfecter of our faith, who for the joy that was set before him endured the cross" (12:2). The future is not the only focus of faith, as the writer will repeatedly tell his readers to look back on the past and finished work of Jesus ("Since then we have a great high priest who has passed through the heavens, Jesus, the Son of God, let us hold fast [in faith, to] our confession," 4:14) and present and continuing work ("Let us . . . [when tempted] with confidence [and in faith] draw near to the throne of grace, that we may receive mercy and find grace to help in time of need," 4:16). But faith certainly is linked with hope, the hope that helps us, as strangers and exiles on earth, to look forward to the rewards that await everyone who considers "the reproach of Christ greater" (11:26) than anything the world offers.

Prayer Prompt

Take time to focus on the past, present, and future aspects of faith. Thank God for the gift of faith and for the great cloud of witnesses—examples and exemplars—who encourage God's people to press on through the arduous race of life, overcoming sin that can stall us and trials that can pull us off course. Pray to Jesus, the "perfecter" of your faith, for the ability to trust God now for the future joys of the city of God, the better heavenly country.

Memory Verse

And without faith it is impossible to please him, for whoever would draw near to God must believe that he exists and that he rewards those who seek him.   *Hebrews 11:6*

• • •

"When Peace Like a River (It Is Well with My Soul)"
Horatio G. Spafford • 1873

When peace, like a river, attendeth my way,
When sorrows like sea billows roll;
Whatever my lot, Thou has taught me to say,
It is well, it is well, with my soul.

REFRAIN
It is well, with my soul,
It is well, it is well, with my soul.

Though Satan should buffet, though trials should come,
Let this blest assurance control,
That Christ has regarded my helpless estate,
And hath shed His own blood for my soul.

REFRAIN

My sin—oh, the bliss of this glorious thought!—
My sin, not in part but the whole,

Is nailed to the cross, and I bear it no more,
Praise the Lord, praise the Lord, O my soul!

REFRAIN

And Lord, haste the day when my faith shall be sight,
The clouds be rolled back as a scroll;
The trump shall resound, and the Lord shall descend,
Even so, it is well with my soul.

REFRAIN

Faith

Part 2 of 5

Adoration
Pray the prayer below. Then pause to praise God for who he is and what he has done.

I believe, O God, that you are an eternal, incomprehensible spirit, infinite in all perfections; who made all things out of nothing and governs them all by your wise providence. I praise you this day my Creator, Sustainer, Redeemer, and Friend. Amen.
Richard Allen

Confession
Pray the prayer below. Then take time to ask God through Jesus to forgive specific sins.

From the time of Adam in the garden you have asked your people to trust in your word. Your call for faith echoes through the ages, from the days of Habakkuk to our present day. Yet, Lord, your people have so often failed to follow in faith. Adam doubted that your boundaries were good and chose not to wait on your good promises, ushering sin into the world. Israel repeatedly grumbled and failed to worship you alone, leading to their exile. Even the Spirit-gifted church today, myself included, wavers in faith, so often succumbing to worries, stresses, and fears. Lord, I admit that I am anxious about today and tomorrow when I should treasure and trust you and concentrate my energies on seeking first your kingdom. Forgive me for my lack of trust. Give me the grace today to cast all my anxieties upon you and to wait faithfully for you to help me. Like you did Habakkuk, guide me as I walk by faith, even on the paths ahead that are shrouded in uncertainty and filled with danger. Amen.   *Based on Habakkuk 2:2–4*

Thanksgiving
Thank God for the truth that "If we confess our sins, he is faithful and just to forgive us our sins and to cleanse us from all unrighteousness" (1 John 1:9), then pray the prayer below. Finally, take time to thank God for specific blessings in your life. Also feel free to offer Psalm 118:1 ("Oh give thanks to the Lord, *for he is good; for his steadfast love endures forever!") as a repeated refrain as you list off (and lift up!) to God people, events, gifts, and circumstances for which you are thankful.*

I will give thanks to the Lord with my whole heart;
    I will recount all of your wonderful deeds.
I will be glad and exult in you;
    I will sing praise to your name, O Most High.   *Psalm 9:1–2*

Supplication
After you pray the prayer below, feel free to add your own specific requests.

Give me a heart to believe, that I may obey you, for you have commanded it. Give me a heart to believe, that I may please you, for you have declared it to be your good pleasure. Give me a heart to believe, that I may honor you, for you have declared that gives glory to you. Amen.   *David Clarkson*

Prayer of Illumination
Blessed Lord, who caused all holy Scriptures to be written for our learning: Grant that I may hear them, read, mark, learn, and

inwardly digest them, that by patience, and the comfort of your holy word, I may embrace, and ever hold fast the blessed hope of everlasting life, which you have given us in our Savior Jesus Christ, who lives and reigns with you and the Holy Spirit, one God, forever and ever. Amen.   Book of Common Prayer (1662)

• • •

Scripture Reading
> I hear, and my body trembles;
>> my lips quiver at the sound;
> rottenness enters into my bones;
>> my legs tremble beneath me.
> Yet I will quietly wait for the day of trouble
>> to come upon people who invade us.
> Though the fig tree should not blossom,
>> nor fruit be on the vines,
> the produce of the olive fail
>> and the fields yield no food,
> the flock be cut off from the fold
>> and there be no herd in the stalls,
> yet I will rejoice in the LORD;
>> I will take joy in the God of my salvation.
> GOD, the Lord, is my strength;
>> he makes my feet like the deer's;
>> he makes me tread on my high places.   Habakkuk 3:16–19

Concise Commentary
There are a number of ways to change the mood or atmosphere of a song. A brilliant example of this is found in Bach's "Crucifixus" from his Mass in B Minor. As the choir sings of Jesus's crucifixion under Pontus Pilate, we hear thirteen repetitions of the diabolical-sounding ground bass. This symbolizes the temporary triumph of evil. However, this evil is danced upon, if you

will, by the harmony, which leads the hearers up and out from the pit, triumphing in the death of death in the death of Christ. Another example is that of the pipe organ when the organist uses a change of registration to effect a change, perhaps from somberness to celebration. A further way to produce an atmospheric shift musically is through a key change. For example, one can go from a lower key in the first three verses of a hymn to a higher key, usually a half step up, in the final verse. Similarly, at the conclusion and climax of Habakkuk's hymn of faith (his "prayer" set to music, "with stringed instruments" to "the choirmaster," 3:1, 19), there is a *poetic* key change. Even more than that, the prophet moves from a minor key to a major key. He does this twice, each time when he strikes the word "yet."[2]

The first major key of faith sounds like this: faith waits for God's righteous wrath. Habakkuk has been told that the cruel Chaldeans are coming, and he reacts in fear. "I hear [they are coming], and [so] my body trembles; my lips quiver at the sound; rottenness enters into my bones; my legs tremble beneath me" (3:16). Just as our Lord's thinking about drinking the cup of God's wrath produced sweat like drops of blood at Gethsemane, so here Habakkuk's fear manifests itself physically, from head to toe, or from lips to legs. But, since he knows God's "work" of wrath in the past, as he states so clearly in verse 2 and then illustrates so thoroughly in verses 3–15, his trembling gives way to trust. "Yet I will quietly wait for the day of trouble to come upon people [these Babylonians] who invade us" (v. 16). He will wait quietly, without complaint. He will wait for God's wrath to fall upon this evil empire. He wants justice!

The second major key, which is expressed beautifully in verses 17–19, reflects how faith rejoices in God, even in adversity. In 2:4 the Lord tells the prophet, "The righteous shall live by his faith." Here that message finds its embodiment as Habakkuk, the righteous man, lives by his steadfast trust in God. We sometimes say or hear others say, "I never could have made it through that without my faith." Well, the prophet would say, more precisely, "I never could have made it through that without my God"—"God, the Lord, is my strength; he makes my feet like the deer's; he makes me tread on my high places." Here, as Habakkuk acknowledges the effects of Israel's apostasy, he also acknowledges his ultimate allegiance. There will be no food. There will be no money. But that matters not, for God alone is his sustenance, and God alone his treasure.

Prayer Prompt
Take time to ask God, through his Spirit, to strengthen your faith—a faith that should express itself through waiting patiently for God's coming judgment and rejoicing in God as your strength and sustenance, even in times of adversity.

> Memory Verse
> And without faith it is impossible to please him, for whoever would draw near to God must believe that he exists and that he rewards those who seek him.   *Hebrews 11:6*

◆ ◆ ◆

"Be Still, My Soul"
Katharina von Schlegel | *trans. Jane Borthwick* • 1855

Be still, my soul; the Lord is on thy side;
bear patiently the cross of grief or pain.
Leave to thy God to order and provide;
in every change He faithful will remain.
Be still, my soul; thy best, thy heav'nly Friend
through thorny ways leads to a joyful end.

Be still, my soul; thy God doth undertake
to guide the future as He has the past.
Thy hope, thy confidence let nothing shake;
all now mysterious shall be bright at last.
Be still, my soul; the waves and winds still know
His voice who ruled them while He dwelt below.

Be still, my soul; when dearest friends depart,
and all is darkened in the veil of tears,
then shalt thou better know His love, His heart,
who comes to soothe thy sorrow and thy fears.
Be still, my soul; thy Jesus can repay
from His own fullness all He takes away.

Be still, my soul; the hour is hast'ning on
when we shall be forever with the Lord,
when disappointment, grief, and fear are gone,
sorrow forgot, love's purest joys restored.
Be still, my soul; when change and tears are past,
all safe and bless-ed we shall meet at last.

Faith

Part 3 of 5

Adoration
Pray the prayer below. Then pause to praise God for who he is and what he has done.

O Holy Father, you have freely given your Son;
O Divine Son, you have freely paid my debt;
O Eternal Spirit, you have freely bid me come;
O Triune God, you do freely grace me with salvation. Amen.
 Valley of Vision[3]

Confession
Pray the prayer below. Then take time to ask God through Jesus to forgive specific sins.

I need to repent of my repentance; I need my tears to be washed; I have no robe to bring to cover my sins, no loom with which to weave my own righteousness. I am always standing clothed in filthy garments and by grace am always receiving change of raiment, for you always justify the ungodly; I am always going into the far country, and always returning home as a prodigal, always saying, Father, forgive me, and you are always bringing forth the best robe. Every morning let me wear it, every evening return in it, go out to the day's work in it, be married in it, be wound in death in it, stand before the great white throne in it, enter heaven in it, shining as the sun. Grant me never to lose sight of the exceeding sinfulness of sin, the exceeding righteousness of salvation, the exceeding glory of Christ, the exceeding beauty of holiness, the exceeding wonder of grace. Amen.   *Valley of Vision*[4]

Thanksgiving

Thank God for the truth that "If we confess our sins, he is faithful and just to forgive us our sins and to cleanse us from all unrighteousness" (1 John 1:9), then pray the prayer below. Finally, take time to thank God for specific blessings in your life. Also feel free to offer Psalm 118:1 ("Oh give thanks to the LORD, *for he is good; for his steadfast love endures forever!") as a repeated refrain as you list off (and lift up!) to God people, events, gifts, and circumstances for which you are thankful.*

Lord God, I come before you with a heart filled with gratitude and praise. In the midst of my distress and despair I called out to you, and you heard my voice. From the great depths I cried out, and you answered my prayer! Your faithfulness knows no bounds. In my darkest hour, where I felt so far from your sight, I clung to the hope of seeing and worshiping you. I thank you for your steadfast love. I offer sacrifices of praise. I sing with real joy and deep gratitude, "Salvation belongs to the Lord!" Amen. *Based on Jonah 2:2–9*

Supplication

After you pray the prayer below, feel free to add your own specific requests.

Hear, O LORD, when I cry aloud;
    be gracious to me and answer me!
You have said, "Seek my face."
My heart says to you,
    "Your face, LORD, do I seek."
    Hide not your face from me.

Turn not your servant away in anger,
O you who have been my help.
Cast me not off; forsake me not,
O God of my salvation!   *Psalm 27:7–9*

Prayer of Illumination
Heavenly Father, I bow in your presence. May your word be my
rule, your Spirit my teacher, and your greater glory my supreme
concern. I ask through Jesus Christ my Lord. Amen.   *John Stott*

◆ ◆ ◆

Scripture Reading
And Jesus went away from there and withdrew to the district
of Tyre and Sidon. And behold, a Canaanite woman from that
region came out and was crying, "Have mercy on me, O Lord,
Son of David; my daughter is severely oppressed by a demon."
But he did not answer her a word. And his disciples came and
begged him, saying, "Send her away, for she is crying out after
us." He answered, "I was sent only to the lost sheep of the house
of Israel." But she came and knelt before him, saying, "Lord, help
me." And he answered, "It is not right to take the children's bread
and throw it to the dogs." She said, "Yes, Lord, yet even the dogs
eat the crumbs that fall from their masters' [Greek: *kyrios*] table."
Then Jesus answered her, "O woman, great is your faith! Be it done
for you as you desire." And her daughter was healed instantly.
Matthew 15:21–28

Concise Commentary
Why would Jesus travel to Tyre and Sidon? Well, as we will see,
he plans there to show the Great Commission before he gives it;
that is, he intends to offer his mercy to people from all nations,
even Canaanites. Matthew uses that archaic title "Canaanite" to
emphasize this point. Jesus will love even Israel's enemies; he

will give grace to those who seem farthest from the kingdom. But notice, in this short narrative, that the woman initiates the action. (In fact, notice her movement toward Jesus throughout. Faith moves toward him!) She comes out of the Gentile region and cries out, "Have mercy on me, O Lord, Son of David; my daughter is severely oppressed by a demon" (15:22). Here she clearly states her problem and trusts that Jesus can offer a solution. She calls him "Lord" and "Son of David," two titles used often in Matthew by people who express faith in Jesus. Even though she is a Gentile, she believes that Jesus is the Messiah, the promised King from David's line, and she believes that Jesus is "Lord" (a title she uses four times!) as she believes Jesus has the divine authority to accomplish her desire and show her family "mercy" through a miracle. Even through the disciples' annoyance with and dismissal of her ("Send her away, for she is crying out after us," 15:23) and Jesus's initial reluctance, she perseveres in faith. Even when Jesus seemingly denies her request (although he likely is testing her faith!) because his mission, as the Jewish Messiah, is to "the lost sheep of the house of Israel" (15:24) and thus it would not be "right to take the children's bread [the promises to Israel] and throw it to the dogs [Gentiles]" (15:25), she turns the theological tables on him before she and her daughter sit down at the messianic banquet. "She said, 'Yes, Lord, yet even the dogs eat the crumbs that fall from their masters' [the Lord's] table'" (15:27). The Lord's "yes" to her "Yes, Lord . . ." follows, coming climactically in the final verse, which emphasizes Jesus's "great faith" commendation and his miraculous provision (15:28).

Just as Jesus miraculously provided bread for the five-thousand-plus Jews (14:13–21) and will provide it for the four-thousand-plus Gentiles or mix of Gentiles and Jews (15:32–38), so here he feeds this woman "crumbs" (15:27) from "the children's bread" (15:26) on the "masters' table" (15:27). But some crumbs! It is as though he pushed the whole fatted calf on the floor: "Her daughter was healed" (15:28). The demon is ousted.

Prayer Prompt

Take time to ask God, through his Spirit, to give you "great faith"—a faith that acknowledges Jesus as the Son of David and Lord, a Savior who came for Jews and Gentiles; a faith that is humble and persistent; a faith that trusts that Jesus has the comprehensive power to offer God's mercy and to provide deliverance from evil.

Memory Verse

And without faith it is impossible to please him, for whoever would draw near to God must believe that he exists and that he rewards those who seek him.   *Hebrews 11:6*

◆ ◆ ◆

"Praise to the Lord, the Almighty, the King of Creation!"
Joachim Neander · *1680* | *trans. Catherine Winkworth* · *1863*

Praise to the Lord, the Almighty, the King of creation!
O my soul, praise him, for he is thy health and salvation!
All ye who hear, now to his temple draw near,
join me in glad adoration.

Praise to the Lord, who o'er all things so wondrously reigneth;
shelters thee under his wings, yea, so gently sustaineth!
Hast thou not seen how thy desires e'er have been
granted in what he ordaineth?

Praise to the Lord, who doth prosper thy work and defend thee;
surely his goodness and mercy here daily attend thee.
Ponder anew what the Almighty will do,
if with his love he befriend thee.

Praise to the Lord! O let all that is in me adore him!
All that hath life and breath, come now with praises before him.
Let the Amen sound from his people again;
gladly fore'er we adore him.

Faith

Part 4 of 5

Adoration

Pray the prayer below. Then pause to praise God for who he is and what he has done.

Father in heaven, I bow before you because I am humbled by your greatness and goodness, and I ask, according to the riches of your glory, that you would grant me strength and power through your Spirit in my inner being. May Christ dwell in my heart through faith, and may I be rooted and grounded in your love. Give me the ability to comprehend something of the immeasurable breadth, length, height, and depth of your love and help me to know that the love of Christ surpasses all knowledge. Fill me with your fullness, O great God, and remind me, even this day, that you can do far more abundantly than all I ask or can imagine. I trust that your power is at work in me, and I pray that you would manifest your glory in the church and in your Son throughout all generations. May your name—Father, Son, and Spirit—be praised and glorified forever and ever and exalted above all. Amen.   *Based on Ephesians 3:14–21*

Confession

Pray the prayer below. Then take time to ask God through Jesus to forgive specific sins.

O Lord, "How many are my iniquities and my sins? Make me know my transgression and my sin" (Job 13:23). Make me know my sins of omission and commission, my intentional and unintentional sins, my sins against you and others, my sins of the heart, mind, and body. Make me know my sins, O Lord, so I might better know your love for me in Jesus Christ; so I might cling to the cross as my only hope for salvation, as the place where your mercy and justice kiss, and the kiss of your mercy, like a "burning coal" that is "taken with tongs from the altar" and placed upon my lips, cleanses me from all my sins, atones for all my iniquities, and removes all my guilt and shame (Isa. 6:6–7). Amen.

Thanksgiving

Thank God for the truth that "If we confess our sins, he is faithful and just to forgive us our sins and to cleanse us from all unrighteousness" (1 John 1:9), then pray the prayer below. Finally, take time to thank God for specific blessings in your life. Also feel free to offer Psalm 118:1 ("Oh give thanks to the LORD, *for he is good; for his steadfast love endures forever!") as a repeated refrain as you list off (and lift up!) to God people, events, gifts, and circumstances for which you are thankful.*

It is good to give thanks to the LORD,
    to sing praises to your name, O Most High;
to declare your steadfast love in the morning,
    and your faithfulness by night,
to the music of the lute and the harp,
    to the melody of the lyre.
For you, O LORD, have made me glad by your work;
    at the works of your hands I sing for joy.   Psalm 92:1–4

Supplication

After you pray the prayer below, feel free to add your own specific requests.

Blessed Lord, have you not again and again said to me, as once the king of Israel said to the king of Syria, "I am yours, and all that I have" (1 Kings 20:4)? You say, "I am yours! My mercy is yours to pardon you. My blood is yours to cleanse you. My merits are yours to justify you. My righteousness is yours to clothe you. My Spirit is yours to lead you. My grace is yours to enrich you. And my glory is yours to reward you." Therefore my gracious soul says, "I cannot but make a resignation of myself to you. Lord, here I am. Do with me as seems good in your own eyes." I know the best way to have my own will is to resign myself to your will, and to say amen to your amen.   *Thomas Brooks*

Prayer of Illumination
O Lord God Almighty, I thank you with all my heart for feeding me with the Bread of Heaven, for man does not live by bread alone but by every word the comes out of your mouth. I ask you now, as I read the Bible, so to illumine my mind with your Holy Spirit that I may increase in faith in you, in certainty of hope in your promises, and in fervency of love to you and my neighbor, to the glory and praise of your holy name. Amen.   *Miles Coverdale*

◆ ◆ ◆

Scripture Reading
And you were dead in the trespasses and sins in which you once walked, following the course of this world, following the prince of the power of the air, the spirit that is now at work in the sons of disobedience—among whom we all once lived in the passions of our flesh, carrying out the desires of the body and the mind, and were by nature children of wrath, like the rest of mankind. But God, being rich in mercy, because of the great love with which he loved us, even when we were dead in our trespasses, made us alive together with Christ—by grace you have been saved— and raised

us up with him and seated us with him in the heavenly places in Christ Jesus, so that in the coming ages he might show the immeasurable riches of his grace in kindness toward us in Christ Jesus. For by grace you have been saved through faith. And this is not your own doing; it is the gift of God, not a result of works, so that no one may boast. For we are his workmanship, created in Christ Jesus for good works, which God prepared beforehand, that we should walk in them. Ephesians 2:1–10

Concise Commentary

What theological treasures are found in these verses! There is so much to digest. However, since our focus here is on faith, we will feed on the first clause from verse 8 ("For by grace you have been saved through faith"). In context the "grace" being described comes from God the Father through Jesus Christ. We "were dead" in our "trespasses and sins," living for the "passions of our flesh" (2:2) and "carrying out the [evil] desires of the body and the mind" (2:3), under the power of the devil ("the prince of the power of the air," 2:2), and thus destined for God's judgment (we "were by nature children of wrath, like the rest of mankind," 2:3). But God stepped in! Because he is "rich in mercy" and because he loves us with "great love," he sent Christ to die for us so we, who "were dead in our trespasses," can be (have been!) "made . . . alive with Christ" (2:4–5). More than that, God has "raised us up" with Christ "and seated us with him in the heavenly places" (2:6). He has done this for us to "show" us forever and ever the "immeasurable riches of his grace in kindness toward us in Christ Jesus" (2:7). Such grace, Paul makes clear, comes through faith ("By grace you have been saved through faith"); such faith is given as a divine gift ("And this is not your own doing; it is the gift of God," 2:8). So, if we are saved by God alone through faith alone, then we cannot boast that it was our good works or keeping the laws of the Old Testament that made God receive us. He worked in us! He gave us faith. He even gave us a faith that works: "For we are his workmanship, created in Christ Jesus for good works, which God prepared beforehand, that we should walk in them" (2:10). What amazing grace!

Prayer Prompt
Take time to ask God to give you a deep understanding and appreciation for the gift of faith. Ask him to free you from ever boasting in yourself, your righteousness, or your good works. And give him now and always the glory that he alone deserves for saving you through faith in Jesus.

Memory Verse
And without faith it is impossible to please him, for whoever would draw near to God must believe that he exists and that he rewards those who seek him.   *Hebrews 11:6*

◆ ◆ ◆

"Amazing Grace"
John Newton • *1779 (st. 1–3)* | *A Collection of Sacred Ballads* • *1790 (st. 4)*

Amazing grace! how sweet the sound
that saved a wretch like me!
I once was lost, but now am found,
was blind, but now I see.

'Twas grace that taught my heart to fear,
and grace my fears relieved;
how precious did that grace appear
the hour I first believed!

Through many dangers, toils, and snares,
I have already come;
'tis grace hath brought me safe thus far,
and grace will lead me home.

When we've been there ten thousand years,
bright shining as the sun,
we've no less days to sing God's praise
than when we'd first begun.

Faith

Part 5 of 5

Adoration
Pray the prayer below. Then pause to praise God for who he is and what he has done.

Blessed are you, O Lord, God of our ancestors,
    and to be praised and highly exalted forever;
Blessed is your glorious, holy name
    and to be highly praised and highly exalted forever;
Blessed are you in the shrine of your holy glory
    and to be extolled and highly glorified forever.
Blessed are you, who sits upon cherubim and looks upon the deeps,
    and to be praised and highly exalted forever.
Blessed are you in the firmament of heaven
    and to be sung and glorified forever.   *Song of the Three Young Men*

Glory to you, Father, Son, and Holy Spirit; I will praise you and highly exalt you forever. Amen.

Confession
Pray the prayer below. Then take time to ask God through Jesus to forgive specific sins.

O merciful Father, regard not what I have done against you, but what our blessed Savior has done for me. Regard not what I have made myself, but what he has made unto me of you, my God. O that Christ may be to me wisdom and righteousness, sanctification and redemption! That his precious blood may cleanse me from all my sins, and that your Holy Spirit may renew and sanctify my soul. May he crucify my flesh with its affections and lusts, and mortify all the parts of my body. O let not sin reign in me—body and soul—that I obey the desires of the fallen flesh, but, being made free from sin through the blood of Christ, let me be the servant of righteousness. Amen.   *John Wesley*

Thanksgiving

Thank God for the truth that "If we confess our sins, he is faithful and just to forgive us our sins and to cleanse us from all unrighteousness" (1 John 1:9), then pray the prayer below. Finally, take time to thank God for specific blessings in your life. Also feel free to offer Psalm 118:1 ("Oh give thanks to the Lord, *for he is good; for his steadfast love endures forever!") as a repeated refrain as you list off (and lift up!) to God people, events, gifts, and circumstances for which you are thankful.*

Blessed be the Lord!
    For he has heard the voice of my pleas for mercy.
The Lord is my strength and my shield;
    in him my heart trusts, and I am helped;
my heart exults,
    and with my song I give thanks to him.   *Psalm 28:6–7*

Supplication

After you pray the prayer below, feel free to add your own specific requests.

Show me your mercy, O Lord, and grant me your salvation. Clothe your ministers with righteousness; let your people sing with joy. Give peace, O Lord, in all the world, for only in you can we live in safety. Lord, keep this nation under your care, and guide us in the way of justice and truth. Let your way be known upon earth, your saving health among all nations. Let not the needy, O Lord, be forgotten, nor the hope of the poor be taken away. Amen.   Book of Common Prayer (1979)

Prayer of Illumination

Lord, you have given your word for a light to shine upon my path; grant me so to meditate on that word, and to follow its teaching, that I may find in it the light that shines more and more until the perfect day; through Jesus Christ our Lord. Amen.   Jerome

• • •

Scripture Reading

What good is it, my brothers, if someone says he has faith but does not have works? Can that faith save him? If a brother or sister is poorly clothed and lacking in daily food, and one of you says to them, "Go in peace, be warmed and filled," without giving them the things needed for the body, what good is that? So also faith by itself, if it does not have works, is dead.

But someone will say, "You have faith and I have works." Show me your faith apart from your works, and I will show you my faith by my works. You believe that God is one; you do well. Even the demons believe—and shudder! Do you want to be shown, you foolish person, that faith apart from works is useless? Was not Abraham our father justified by works when he offered up his son Isaac on the altar? You see that faith was active along with his works, and faith was completed by his works; and the Scripture was fulfilled that says, "Abraham believed God, and it was counted to him as righteousness"—and he was called a friend of God. You see that a person is justified by works and not by faith alone. And in the same way was not also Rahab the prostitute justified by works when she received the messengers and sent them out by another way? For as the body apart from the spirit is dead, so also faith apart from works is dead.   James 2:14–26

Concise Commentary

James begins with two questions: "What good is it, my brothers, if someone says he has faith but does not have works? Can that faith save him?" (2:16–17). His answer is no: "Faith apart from works is useless" (2:20). A faith that saves, or saving faith, should be obvious and visible, and, when James announces "Show me your faith!" (2:18), he makes clear what saving faith looks like. In verses 1–13 he speaks of a faith that loves and in verses 14–26 of a faith that works. James does not claim that we must have good works instead of faith or mere intellectual assent to the tenets of Christianity without good works; rather, we must have faith and works or *a faith that works*. Put differently, he is not contrasting faith with works or works with faith, but rather is contrasting two types of faith. One type is a dead faith, a faith without works ("faith by itself, if it does not have works, is dead," 2:17; cf. 2:26); the other type is a living faith, a faith with works ("faith . . . active along with . . . works," 2:22). In verses 14–19 he offers two illustrations of the dead faith of a professing Christian: first, when someone encounters a Christian in physical need and responds with words not works; second, when someone holds to orthodox theology (believes "that God is one," 2:19) without works. Such is the faith of demons ("Even the demons believe—and shudder!," 2:19)! Then in verses 20–26 he offers two illustrations of a living faith, that of Abraham and Rahab. He was a man; she was a woman. He a Jew; she a Gentile. He rich; she poor. He a patriarch; she a prostitute. Yet what they had in common was a living faith: Abraham "offered up his son Isaac on the altar" (2:21); Rahab "received the messengers and sent them out by another way" (2:25). We are not saved by good works, but we cannot be saved without them. That is—and to return to the previous devotion on Ephesians 2—we are "saved through faith" and not as a "result of works" (Eph. 2:8–9), and yet, once we are saved, our faith works. Why? Because we are God's "workmanship, created in Christ Jesus for good works, which God prepared beforehand [he gives faith; he gives works], that we should walk in them" (Eph. 2:10).

Prayer Prompt
Take time to thank God for the gift of living faith. Ask him so to strengthen your faith that it manifests itself regularly in love for others and in good deeds. As you wait for "the appearing of the glory of our great God and Savior Jesus Christ, who gave himself to redeem us from all lawlessness," pray that he would make you "zealous for good works" (Titus 2:13–14).

Memory Verse
And without faith it is impossible to please him, for whoever would draw near to God must believe that he exists and that he rewards those who seek him.   *Hebrews 11:6*

◆ ◆ ◆

"I Bind Unto Myself Today"
Attributed to Patrick of Ireland • 387–493 | Tune: St. Patrick • 1902

Refrain Tune

I bind unto myself today
the strong name of the Trinity,
by invocation of the same
the Three in One and One in Three.

I bind this today to me forever
by power of faith, Christ's incarnation;
his baptism in Jordan river,
his death on cross for my salvation;
his bursting from the spicèd tomb,
his riding up the heavenly way,
his coming at the day of doom
I bind unto myself today.

REFRAIN
Christ be with me, Christ within me,
Christ behind me, Christ before me,
Christ beside me, Christ to win me,
Christ to comfort and restore me.
Christ beneath me, Christ above me,
Christ in quiet, Christ in danger,
Christ in hearts of all that love me,
Christ in mouth of friend and stranger.

I bind unto myself the name,
the strong name of the Trinity,
by invocation of the same,
the Three in One and One in Three.
By whom all nature hath creation,
Eternal Father, Spirit, Word:
praise to the Lord of my salvation,
salvation is of Christ the Lord.

Love

Part 1 of 5

Through these biblical and ancient Christian prayers offer your adoration and gratitude to God, confess your sins, and ask for help to read his word and live the Christian life. If it helps, pray aloud and with physical gestures, such as raising your hands (1 Tim. 2:8) when you praise God's holy name or kneeling (Dan. 6:10) or lying prostrate (Luke 5:8) when you confess your sins. Using different postures to pray can engage your body and mind in new ways! "Stand up and bless the LORD your God from everlasting to everlasting" (Neh. 9:5).

Gloria Patri
Pray the Gloria Patri. Then take time to praise and thank God for specific blessings in your life.

Glory be to the Father, and to the Son, and to the Holy Ghost,
As it was in the beginning, is now, and ever shall be,
    world without end.
Amen.

Agnus Dei
Pray the Agnus Dei. Then take time to ask God through Jesus to forgive specific sins. Also offer prayers of lament. Pray that God would deal with sufferings and injustices both now and when Christ returns. Cry out, "O Sovereign

Lord, holy and true, how long before you will judge and avenge our blood on those who dwell on the earth?" (Rev. 6:10), or "Out of the depths I cry to you, O Lord! O Lord, hear my voice! Let your ears be attentive to the voice of my pleas for mercy!" (Ps. 130:1–2).

Lamb of God, who takes away the sins of the world,
 have mercy on us.
Lamb of God, who takes away the sins of the world,
 have mercy on us.
Lamb of God, who takes away the sins of the world,
 grant us peace. Amen.

The Lord's Prayer
Pray each line slowly. As you think about each petition, add your own specific requests.

Our Father in heaven,
hallowed be your name.
Your kingdom come,
your will be done,
 on earth as it is in heaven.
Give us this day our daily bread,
and forgive us our debts,
 as we also have forgiven our debtors.
And lead us not into temptation,
 but deliver us from evil. Matthew 6:9–13

Prayer of Illumination
The words of the Lord are pure words,
 like silver refined in a furnace on the ground,
  purified seven times. Psalm 12:6

Lord, I humbly ask that you would refine my heart and mind through your pure and perfect word. And may your words of love be a source of encouragement and transformation in my life. Amen.

• • •

Scripture Reading

Hear, O Israel: The LORD our God, the LORD is one. You shall love the LORD your God with all your heart and with all your soul and with all your might. And these words that I command you today shall be on your heart. You shall teach them diligently to your children, and shall talk of them when you sit in your house, and when you walk by the way, and when you lie down, and when you rise. You shall bind them as a sign on your hand, and they shall be as frontlets between your eyes. You shall write them on the doorposts of your house and on your gates.   *Deuteronomy 6:4–9*

Concise Commentary

The Lord God gave Israel the Shema (from the Hebrew word for "hear") as he brought them into the promised land ("a land flowing with milk and honey," Deut. 6:3). The Shema starts with a confession, followed by a command. The confession is that God is one, and the command is to love the one and only God with the whole of who we are—heart (our emotions, but also our intellect), soul (our entire being), and strength (our abilities and actions). Since Yahweh is one, our complete ("all" [3x]—all of who we are) adoration and allegiance are to him. Total Godward devotion. "Love," this all-encompassing word, involves all of us—our attitudes, affections, and actions.

When Jesus is asked, "Which commandment is the most important [protos] of all?"—first among all the commandments?—(Mark 12:28), he replies, "The most important is, 'Hear, O Israel: The Lord our God, the Lord is one. And you shall love the Lord your God with all your heart and with all your soul and with all your mind and with all your strength.' The second is this: 'You shall love your neighbor as yourself.' There is no other commandment greater than these" (12:29–31). Notice that he adds "all your mind," perhaps to emphasize and include the intellect or merely to clarify in his context that every human faculty is included. He also includes the commandment from Leviticus 19:18. Jesus adds this second commandment ("You shall love your neighbor as yourself") because the first cannot exist without it. This is why Jesus says, "There is no other commandment [singular] greater than these [plural]" (Mark 12:31). The two are one great commandment. As the apostle John writes, "If anyone says, 'I love God,' and hates his brother, he is a liar; for he who does not love his brother whom he has seen cannot love God whom he has not seen" (1 John 4:20). To love God is to love people; to love people is to love God. In this way the Christian life mirrors Christ's cross. There is a vertical dimension (love for God) that connects with a horizontal (love for others).[5]

Prayer Prompt
Take time to ask God, through his Spirit, to help you love him and love others. Pray specifically for those people in your life who are difficult to love. Ask God to open your heart, head, and hands to extend the love you have been given by God to them.

Memory Verse
For I am sure that neither death nor life, nor angels nor rulers, nor things present nor things to come, nor powers, nor height nor depth, nor anything else in all creation, will be able to separate us from the love of God in Christ Jesus our Lord.   *Romans 8:38–39*

• • •

"What Wondrous Love Is This"
Anonymous · 1811

What wondrous love is this, O my soul, O my soul!
What wondrous love is this, O my soul!
What wondrous love is this, that caused the Lord of bliss
to bear the dreadful curse for my soul, for my soul,
to bear the dreadful curse for my soul.

When I was sinking down, sinking down, sinking down,
when I was sinking down, O my soul!
When I was sinking down beneath God's righteous frown,
Christ laid aside His crown for my soul, for my soul,
Christ laid aside His crown for my soul.

To God and to the Lamb I will sing, I will sing;
to God and to the Lamb, I will sing.
To God and to the Lamb who is the great "I AM,"
while millions join the theme, I will sing, I will sing,
while millions join the theme, I will sing.

And when from death I'm free, I'll sing on, I'll sing on,
and when from death I'm free, I'll sing on.
And when from death I'm free, I'll sing and joyful be,
and through eternity, I'll sing on, I'll sing on,
and through eternity I'll sing on.

Love

Part 2 of 5

Adoration

Pray the prayer below. Then pause to praise God for who he is and what he has done.

Shout for joy to God, all the earth;
    sing the glory of his name;
    give to him glorious praise!
Say to God, "How awesome are your deeds!
    So great is your power that your enemies come cringing
        to you.
All the earth worships you
    and sings praises to you;
    they sing praises to your name."   Psalm 66:1–4

Confession

Pray the prayer below. Then take time to ask God through Jesus to forgive specific sins.

Lord God, how often I, like Israel of old, act presumptuously and refuse to obey your commandments, forgetting all that you have done for me and desiring to return to slavery to sin, as Israel longed to return to its slavery in Egypt. But, Father, you are a God ready to forgive, gracious and merciful, slow to anger and abounding in steadfast love. So forgive my forgetfulness, rebellion, and blasphemies and destroy any and all idols in my life. Save me from myself! Save me from my sins. Save me from my enemies. Deliver me from all evil. I love you, Lord, for you are a gracious and merciful God. Amen.   Based on Nehemiah 9

Thanksgiving

Thank God for the truth that "If we confess our sins, he is faithful and just to forgive us our sins and to cleanse us from all unrighteousness" (1 John 1:9), then pray the prayer below. Finally, take time to thank God for specific blessings in your life. Also feel free to offer Psalm 118:1 ("Oh give thanks to the Lord, *for he is good; for his steadfast love endures forever!") as a repeated refrain as you list off (and lift up!) to God people, events, gifts, and circumstances for which you are thankful.*

Lord, you have commanded your people through your word to give thanks in all circumstances, for such is your will for us in Christ. But, while I admit how easy it is to rejoice in your gospel and the good news of our salvation and to rejoice when I see all things working together for my good, I also admit how hard it is to give thanks when I cannot see through the storm. So, help me, O Lord, to see through my trials, to have a divine perspective on them, to see them as you see them, and thus to trust in you so that I would indeed rejoice and give thanks even now. Amen.

Supplication

After you pray the prayer below, feel free to add your own specific requests.

Lord, because you have made me, I owe you the whole of my love; because you have redeemed me, I owe you the whole of myself; because you have promised so much, I owe you my whole being. I pray you, Lord, to make me taste by love what I taste by knowledge; let me know by love what I know by understanding. I owe you more than my whole self, but I have no more, and by myself

I cannot render the whole of it to you. Draw me to you, Lord, in the fullness of your love. I am wholly yours by creation; make me all yours, too, in love. Amen.   *Anselm*

Prayer of Illumination
Teach me your way, O LORD,
   that I may walk in your truth;
   unite my heart to fear your name.   *Psalm 86:11*

• • •

Scripture Reading
Beloved, let us love one another, for love is from God, and whoever loves has been born of God and knows God. Anyone who does not love does not know God, because God is love. In this the love of God was made manifest among us, that God sent his only Son into the world, so that we might live through him. In this is love, not that we have loved God but that he loved us and sent his Son to be the propitiation for our sins. Beloved, if God so loved us, we also ought to love one another. No one has ever seen God; if we love one another, God abides in us and his love is perfected in us.   *1 John 4:7–12*

Concise Commentary
In the Bible we often read about something that "God is." Sometimes these words tell us *whom God is with*, as in Genesis 21:20. Often the clause reports *something that God is doing*, as in those many verses in which an Israelite reminds the rest of the people about the "good land that the LORD our God is giving us" (e.g., Deut. 1:25). And sometimes the words tell us *something about what God is or is not like* (e.g., "God is not man," Num. 23:19; "God is a consuming fire," Deut. 4:24; "God is one," Gal. 3:20). Some of the most memorable examples of this last group come from the apostle John: "God is spirit" (John 4:24),

"God is light" (1 John 1:5), and "God is love" (4:8, 16). Regarding "God is love," John is not saying that love is a quality that God possesses; rather, he is saying that love is the essence of God's divine being. The eternal love between the Father, Son, and Spirit that existed before creation spills over into his creation, as God perpetually gives of himself for the benefit of his creation. As John goes on to explain, God's love finds its ultimate expression in Christ's incarnation ("God sent his only Son into the world," 4:9; "Jesus Christ has come in the flesh," 4:2) and crucifixion ("He loved us and sent his Son to be the propitiation for our sins," 4:10; "By this we know love, that he laid down his life for us," 3:16). Through Jesus's propitiatory *death* he removed the guilt of our sins, appeased God's wrath, and gave us eternal *life*—we "live through him" (4:9). Part of living through Jesus is living a life of love for others. Those who are ingrafted into Christ through the Spirit love ("whoever loves has been born of God," 4:7), and, when we love God and others, God's "love is perfected in us" (4:12), that is, God's love for us is made whole and reaches its goal.[6]

Prayer Prompt
Take time to ask God, through the Spirit, to help you to understand better his essence and attribute of love. Ask that the truths that God is love and that he has loved us in Christ would help motivate you to be a loving person who loves others for their good and God's glory.

Memory Verse
For I am sure that neither death nor life, nor angels nor rulers, nor things present nor things to come, nor powers, nor height nor depth, nor anything else in all creation, will be able to separate us from the love of God in Christ Jesus our Lord.   Romans 8:38–39

• • •

"And Can It Be That I Should Gain?"
Charles Wesley • *1738*

And can it be that I should gain
An int'rest in the Saviour's blood?
Died he for me, who caused his pain?
For me, who him to death pursued?
Amazing love! how can it be
That thou, my God, shouldst die for me?
Amazing love! how can it be
That thou, my God, shouldst die for me!

'Tis mystery all! The Immortal dies!
Who can explore his strange design?
In vain the first-born seraph tries
To sound the depths of love divine!
'Tis mercy all! let earth adore,
Let angel minds inquire no more.
'Tis mercy all! let earth adore,
Let angel minds inquire no more.

He left his Father's throne above,
So free, so infinite his grace;
Emptied himself of all but love,
And bled for Adam's helpless race;
'Tis mercy all, immense and free;
For, O my God, it found out me.
'Tis mercy all, immense and free;
For, O my God, it found out me.

Long my imprisoned spirit lay
Fast bound in sin and nature's night;
Thine eye diffused a quickening ray—,
I woke, the dungeon flamed with light;
My chains fell off, my heart was free;
I rose, went forth and followed thee.
My chains fell off, my heart was free;
I rose, went forth and followed thee.

No condemnation now I dread;
Jesus, and all in him is mine!
Alive in him, my living Head,
And clothed in righteousness divine,
Bold I approach the eternal throne,
And claim the crown, through Christ my own.
Bold I approach the eternal throne,
And claim the crown, through Christ my own.

13

Love

Part 3 of 5

Adoration
Pray the prayer below. Then pause to praise God for who he is and what he has done.

Holy, Holy, Holy, Lord God Sabaoth [of the armies of heaven];
Heaven and earth are full of your glory;
Hosanna in the highest.
Blessed is he that comes in the Name of the Lord;
Hosanna in the highest. Amen.   *Sanctus*

Confession
Pray the prayer below. Then take time to ask God through Jesus to forgive specific sins.

I cry out to you, O Lord; have mercy on me, a sinner, and forgive me. My Redeemer, I have sinned and turned from you. Lord, save me, a sinner, and forgive me. King of Heaven and eternal Lord, receive the prayer I pour out before you, and forgive me. Gracious God, in your kindness and through your church visit the sick, release the captives, provide for the widow and orphan, and Lord, have mercy on me, a sinner, and forgive me for my lack of care and compassion. Amen.   *Mozarabic Breviary*

Thanksgiving

Thank God for the truth that "If we confess our sins, he is faithful and just to forgive us our sins and to cleanse us from all unrighteousness" (1 John 1:9), then pray the prayer below. Finally, take time to thank God for specific blessings in your life. Also feel free to offer Psalm 118:1 ("Oh give thanks to the LORD, for he is good; for his steadfast love endures forever!") as a repeated refrain as you list off (and lift up!) to God people, events, gifts, and circumstances for which you are thankful.

All good gifts around us
Are sent from heaven above;
Then thank the Lord, O thank the Lord,
For all his love. Amen.   *Matthias Claudius*

Supplication

After you pray the prayer below, feel free to add your own specific requests.

O good Shepherd, seek me and bring me home to your fold again. I am like the man on the road to Jericho who was attacked by robbers, wounded and left half dead. You who are the Good Samaritan, lift me up and deal favorably with me according to your good pleasure, until I may dwell in your house all the days of my life and praise you for ever and ever with those who are there. Amen.   *Jerome*

Prayer of Illumination

My Lord and God, as I now read your word, soften my heart that I may see your ways. Fill me with your light. Through Jesus Christ I pray. Amen.   *Worship Sourcebook*[7]

• • •

Scripture Reading

But he [a lawyer], desiring to justify himself, said to Jesus, "And who is my neighbor?" Jesus replied, "A man was going down from Jerusalem to Jericho, and he fell among robbers, who stripped him and beat him and departed, leaving him half dead. Now by chance a priest was going down that road, and when he saw him he passed by on the other side. So likewise a Levite, when he came to the place and saw him, passed by on the other side. But a Samaritan, as he journeyed, came to where he was, and when he saw him, he had compassion. He went to him and bound up his wounds, pouring on oil and wine. Then he set him on his own animal and brought him to an inn and took care of him. And the next day he took out two denarii and gave them to the innkeeper, saying, 'Take care of him, and whatever more you spend, I will repay you when I come back.' Which of these three, do you think, proved to be a neighbor to the man who fell among the robbers?" He said, "The one who showed him mercy." And Jesus said to him, "You go, and do likewise." *Luke 10:29–37*

Concise Commentary

From the three major characters in Jesus's parable—a priest, a Levite, and a Samaritan—we can learn two major lessons. From what the two Jewish religious professionals did and did not do we derive our first lesson: Do not let *"divine interruptions"* (what Jesus *ironically labels "by chance"*) *interrupt our worship of the divine.* I word the lesson this way because these two un-neighborly men are returning from worshiping Yahweh in Jerusalem (leading God's *mercy* ministries, no less!) when they ignore a dying man on their way to Jericho. In the temple the priests performed the sacrifices necessary to demonstrate God's mercy upon sinners. The Levites were the temple liturgists, organizing and leading music. Now, the priest could have used the excuse, based on Leviticus 21, that the mugged man was ceremonially unclean because he had died. A priest could not touch a dead body. But Luke makes it clear that the man is not "dead" but "half-dead." We all know that there is a difference between a dead man and a half-dead man: a half-dead man is breathing, and here bleeding and likely moaning or crying out for help. And, even if the man was two seconds from death (or would die in his arms), the higher duty of trying to save a life certainly supersedes any claim to ceremonial lawfulness, as Jesus himself demonstrated throughout his healing ministry. Whatever the priest's excuse (and the Levite's as well), it is absolutely inexcusable!

The second lesson, based on the attitude and actions of the Samaritan, is to *Go and do likewise*. His attitude of mercy ("he had compassion" when he saw the man who was robbed) led to his actions of mercy. Unlike the uncaring clergy, this helpful hero (a Samaritan no less!) provides the comprehensive health-care package. He applies the ancient first aid himself and then pays for all the costs. He cleans, disinfects, and bandages the man's wounds; brings him to an inn; and continues to nurse him back to health throughout the night. Then, the next day, he gives the innkeeper money to cover the costs and says to him, "Take care of him, and whatever more you spend, I will repay you when I come back" (Luke 10:35). It sounds like he is a busy man. He has somewhere to go. But he is not too busy to stop and save a life. We are to go and do likewise, that is, we are to have compassion in our hearts for those in need and demonstrate that love through sacrificial care.

Prayer Prompt

Take time to praise God for Jesus, who did not merely cross a road but traversed a cosmic distance from heaven to earth; who came to us when we were not merely dying but dead in our trespasses and sins; who gave more than a couple of coins from his pocket to gain our salvation, offering the very blood of his body and the agonies of his soul on the cross. Thank Jesus that he

traveled a much greater distance, to help people in much greater
need, at a much greater cost.   *Philip Graham Ryken*

Memory Verse
For I am sure that neither death nor life, nor angels nor rulers,
nor things present nor things to come, nor powers, nor height nor
depth, nor anything else in all creation, will be able to separate
us from the love of God in Christ Jesus our Lord.   *Romans 8:38–39*

• • •

"I Will Sing of My Redeemer"
Philip Paul Bliss · 1876

I will sing of my Redeemer
and his wondrous love to me;
on the cru-el cross he suffered,
from the curse to set me free.
Sing, O sing of my Redeemer!
With his blood he purchased me;
on the cross he sealed my pardon,
paid the debt, and made me free.

I will tell the wondrous story,
how my lost estate to save,
in his boundless love and mercy,
he the ransom freely gave.
I will praise my dear Redeemer,
his triumphant power I'll tell:
how the victory he gives me
over sin and death and hell.

I will sing of my Redeemer
and his heavenly love for me;
he from death to life has brought me,
Son of God, with him to be.
Sing, O sing of my Redeemer!
With his blood he purchased me;
on the cross he sealed my pardon,
paid the debt, and made me free.

Love

Part 4 of 5

Adoration

Pray the prayer below. Then pause to praise God for who he is and what he has done.

"The Lord reigns, let the earth rejoice; let the many coastlands be glad! Clouds and thick darkness are all around him; righteousness and justice are the foundation of his throne" (Ps. 97:1–2). My great and sovereign God, I bow before you now and recognize your righteousness and justice, your holiness and love. And I acknowledge that you alone are worthy to be praised. So I lift my voice and heart in praise of you! Amen.

Confession

Pray the prayer below. Then take time to ask God through Jesus to forgive specific sins.

Blessed is the one whose transgression is forgiven,
    whose sin is covered.
Blessed is the man against whom the Lord counts no iniquity,
    and in whose spirit there is no deceit.

For when I kept silent, my bones wasted away
    through my groaning all day long.

For day and night your hand was heavy upon me;
　　my strength was dried up as by the heat of summer.

I acknowledged my sin to you,
　　and I did not cover my iniquity;
I said, "I will confess my transgressions to the LORD,"
　　and you forgave the iniquity of my sin.　　Psalm 32:1–5

Thanksgiving
Thank God for the truth that "If we confess our sins, he is faithful and just to forgive us our sins and to cleanse us from all unrighteousness" (1 John 1:9), then pray the prayer below. Finally, take time to thank God for specific blessings in your life. Also feel free to offer Psalm 118:1 ("Oh give thanks to the LORD, for he is good; for his steadfast love endures forever!") as a repeated refrain as you list off (and lift up!) to God people, events, gifts, and circumstances for which you are thankful.

Almighty God, Father of all mercies, I, your unworthy servant, give you humble thanks for all your goodness and loving-kindness to me and to all whom you have made. I bless you for your creation, preservation, and all the blessings of this life, but above all for your immeasurable love in the redemption of the world by the Lord Jesus Christ, for the means of grace, and for the hope of glory. And, I pray, give me such an awareness of your mercies that with truly thankful heart I may show forth your praise, not only with my lips but in my life, giving up myself to your service and walking before you in holiness and righteousness all my days; through Jesus Christ, to whom, with you and the Holy Spirit, be honor and glory throughout all ages. Amen.
Book of Common Prayer (1662)

Supplication
After you pray the prayer below, feel free to add your own specific requests.

Fill my heart with your Holy Spirit, and take up your residence there. Dwell in me, walk with me, and let my body be the temple of the Holy Spirit. May I so wait upon the Lord as to renew my strength and go on from one degree of faith, love, zeal, and holiness, to another, until I appear perfect before you through Jesus Christ my Lord, in whom I have righteousness and strength. Amen.   *Philip Doddridge*

Prayer of Illumination

Lord God, you said at creation, "Let light shine out of darkness," and you have, through the Holy Spirit, shone in my heart to give me faith—"the light of the knowledge of the glory of God in the face of Jesus Christ" (2 Cor. 4:6). Today I ask, O Lord, that you would shine down your light from heaven so that I might see the glorious riches of your word. Amen.

. . .

Scripture Reading

If I speak in the tongues of men and of angels, but have not love, I am a noisy gong or a clanging cymbal. And if I have prophetic powers, and understand all mysteries and all knowledge, and if I have all faith, so as to remove mountains, but have not love, I am nothing. If I give away all I have, and if I deliver up my body to be burned, but have not love, I gain nothing.

Love is patient and kind; love does not envy or boast; it is not arrogant or rude. It does not insist on its own way; it is not irritable or resentful; it does not rejoice at wrongdoing, but rejoices with the truth. Love bears all things, believes all things, hopes all things, endures all things.

Love never ends. As for prophecies, they will pass away; as for tongues, they will cease; as for knowledge, it will pass away. For we know in part and we prophesy in part, but when the perfect comes, the partial will pass away. When I was a child, I spoke like a child, I thought like a child, I reasoned like a child. When I became a man, I gave up childish ways. For now we see in a mirror dimly, but then face to face. Now I know in part; then I shall know fully, even as I have been fully known.

So now faith, hope, and love abide, these three; but the greatest of these is love.   1 Corinthians 13

Concise Commentary

At the beginning of Paul's beautiful reflections on love he writes of how being a person full of love is more important than anything else we could do. We can have the most amazing gifts (like faith to move mountains!) and be the most generous person (giving all our money to help others), but, if we do not have love, then all our gifting and giving are worthless. In the middle Paul writes of how love must shape our thoughts, feelings, and actions. For example, love makes us patient and kind with others, and love keeps us from bragging to others about how amazing we are. At the end Paul reflects, "Now faith, hope, and love abide, these three; but the greatest of these is love" (1 Cor. 13:13). Love is greater because love will last! We need faith and hope only until we get to heaven. But in heaven all we will need (and think, feel, and do) is love! There God, who "is love" (1 John 4:8), will love us and we will love him and others all the time for the rest of time.

As you may know (and should know!), Paul's beautiful chapter about love is actually a rebuke. The Christians in Corinth were not loving each other. Some were not sharing food at the Lord's Supper; others were saying terrible things about Paul; still others were celebrating when other Christians sinned. And so Paul shows them, through this chapter, a better way to live— the loving way. When we read this chapter, we probably feel the rebuke too. None of us loves perfectly. So how can we love like this? First John answers this for us: "We love because [God] first loved us" (4:19). We are able to love only when we have known

God's love. The more we know God's love, the better we will be able to love. John 3:16 says, "God so loved the world that he gave his only Son, that whoever believes in him should not perish but have eternal life." That means that the way to know God's love is to know the gospel. Jesus died for us. The more we grasp our sin, the more we grasp what Jesus did when he died for our sins and the more we will love like Jesus did.

Prayer Prompt
Take time to ask God, through his Spirit, to make you a person of love, a Christian who so loves God and so longs for the eternal life of love in heaven that you love your neighbor, and even your enemies, as you love yourself.

> Memory Verse
> For I am sure that neither death nor life, nor angels nor rulers, nor things present nor things to come, nor powers, nor height nor depth, nor anything else in all creation, will be able to separate us from the love of God in Christ Jesus our Lord.   *Romans 8:38–39*

· · ·

"Jesus, Lover of My Soul"
Charles Wesley · 1740[8]

Jesus, lover of my soul,
let me to thy bosom fly,
while the nearer waters roll,
while the tempest still is high;
hide me, O my Savior, hide,
till the storm of life is past;

safe into the haven guide,
O receive my soul at last!

Other refuge have I none;
hangs my helpless soul on thee;
leave, ah! leave me not alone,
still support and comfort me.
All my trust on thee is stayed,
all my help from thee I bring;
cover my defenseless head
with the shadow of thy wing.

Plenteous grace with thee is found,
grace to cover all my sin;
let the healing streams abound;
make and keep me pure within.
Thou of life the fountain art;
freely let me take of thee;
spring thou up within my heart,
rise to all eternity.

Love

Part 5 of 5

Adoration

Pray the prayer below. Then pause to praise God for who he is and what he has done.

The LORD is my strength and my song,
    and he has become my salvation;
this is my God, and I will praise him,
    my father's God, and I will exalt him.   Exodus 15:2

Confession

Pray the prayer below. Then take time to ask God through Jesus to forgive specific sins.

I, a poor sinner, confess before you, my God and Creator, that I have sinned against you grievously in many ways, not only by gross outward sins but much more through inward natural blindness, unbelief, doubts, despondency, impatience, pride, covetousness, secret envy, hatred, malice, and other sinful affections that you see in me, my Lord and God, and that, sadly, I cannot always see in myself. I repent of these and cry to you for your mercy through your beloved Son, Jesus Christ. Amen.
Palatinate Liturgy (1563); Lutheran Liturgy of Württemberg (1536)

Thanksgiving

Thank God for the truth that "If we confess our sins, he is faithful and just to forgive us our sins and to cleanse us from all unrighteousness" (1 John 1:9), then pray the prayer below. Finally, take time to thank God for specific blessings in your life. Also feel free to offer Psalm 118:1 ("Oh give thanks to the LORD, for he is good; for his steadfast love endures forever!") as a repeated refrain as you list off (and lift up!) to God people, events, gifts, and circumstances for which you are thankful.

Give thanks to the LORD, for he is good,
    for his steadfast love endures forever.
Give thanks to the God of gods,
    for his steadfast love endures forever.
Give thanks to the Lord of lords,
    for his steadfast love endures forever;
to him who alone does great wonders,
    for his steadfast love endures forever;
to him who by understanding made the heavens,
    for his steadfast love endures forever;
to him who spread out the earth above the waters,
    for his steadfast love endures forever;
to him who made the great lights,
    for his steadfast love endures forever;
the sun to rule over the day,
    for his steadfast love endures forever;
the moon and stars to rule over the night,
    for his steadfast love endures forever.

It is he who remembered us in our low estate,
    for his steadfast love endures forever;
and rescued us from our foes,
    for his steadfast love endures forever;
he who gives food to all flesh,
    for his steadfast love endures forever.

Give thanks to the God of heaven,
for his steadfast love endures forever.   Psalm 136:1–9, 23–26

Supplication
After you pray the prayer below, feel free to add your own specific requests.

Lord, I yield. I am overcome. O blessed conquest! Go on victoriously, and still prevail, and triumph in your love. This captive of love will proclaim your victory when you lead me in triumph from earth to heaven, from death to life, from the tribunal to the throne. Myself, and all that see it, will acknowledge that you have prevailed, and all will say, "Behold, how he loved him!" Let neither life nor death, nor anything separate me from your love, that I shall be kept in the fullness of love forever. Amen.   *Richard Baxter*

Prayer of Illumination
Transcribe those sacred words on my heart that by your inspiration are recorded in your holy word. Amen.   *Richard Baxter*

. . .

Scripture Reading
What then shall we say to these things? If God is for us, who can be against us? He who did not spare his own Son but gave him up for us all, how will he not also with him graciously give us all things? Who shall bring any charge against God's elect? It is God who justifies. Who is to condemn? Christ Jesus is the one who died—more than that, who was raised—who is at the right hand of God, who indeed is interceding for us. Who shall separate us from the love of Christ? Shall tribulation, or distress, or persecution, or famine, or nakedness, or danger, or sword? As it is written,

"For your sake we are being killed all the day long;
we are regarded as sheep to be slaughtered."

No, in all these things we are more than conquerors through him who loved us. For I am sure that neither death nor life, nor angels nor rulers, nor things present nor things to come, nor powers, nor height nor depth, nor anything else in all creation, will be able to separate us from the love of God in Christ Jesus our Lord.   *Romans 8:31–39*

Concise Commentary

In the first seven chapters of Romans Paul explains how we are saved. We are all sinners. Jesus died for sinners. Those who believe in Jesus are made right with God. And Jesus gives the Spirit to those who believe, to help us follow God's ways. Now, when we get to Romans 8, Paul writes of how we are kept safe in Jesus. First, he makes this marvelous promise: "There is no condemnation for those who are in Christ Jesus" (Rom 8:1). God will not judge us as sinners, because Jesus died for sinners. He took on the punishment we deserve. Second, Paul explains that this world can be compared to a woman's giving birth. There is a lot of groaning and pain, but something good is coming soon. Our present suffering paves the way for a far better future glory.

Lastly, Paul ends with some of the most beautiful words in the Bible, exulting in God's always-and-forever love for us in Jesus: "If God is for us, who can be against us? He who did not spare his own Son but gave him up for us all, how will he not also with him graciously give us all things? How can anyone condemn us if Jesus died for us and now intercedes in heaven for us?" (see 8:31–34). So, can troubles on this earth separate us from the love of God in Christ? No! Persecution or pain? No! Dangers or distresses? No! Demons or death? No! Nothing "will be able to separate us from the love of God in Christ Jesus our Lord" (8:39). So, whatever difficult trials you are experiencing, know that they cannot separate you from God's love for you in Jesus. And, if the all-powerful God loves us, we can trust that everything that happens to us—even the worst sufferings—our always-good God is using to work for our good. What great comfort!

Prayer Prompt

Take time to ask God, through his Spirit, to remind you of his steadfast love for you in Christ, and be grateful for such love now and forever!

Memory Verse

For I am sure that neither death nor life, nor angels nor rulers, nor things present nor things to come, nor powers, nor height nor depth, nor anything else in all creation, will be able to separate us from the love of God in Christ Jesus our Lord.   *Romans 8:38–39*

• • •

"O the Deep, Deep Love of Jesus"
S. Trevor Francis • *1875*

O the deep, deep love of Jesus,
vast, unmeasured, boundless, free,
rolling as a mighty ocean
in its fullness over me.
Underneath me, all around me,
is the current of Thy love;
leading onward, leading homeward
to Thy glorious rest above.

O the deep, deep love of Jesus,
spread His praise from shore to shore!
How He loveth, ever loveth,
changeth never, nevermore!
How He watcheth o'er His loved ones,
died to call them all His own;

how for them He intercedeth,
watcheth o'er them from the throne.

O the deep, deep love of Jesus,
love of every love the best;
'tis an ocean vast of blessing,
'tis a haven sweet of rest.
O the deep, deep love of Jesus,
'tis a heav'n of heav'ns to me;
and it lifts me up to glory,
for it lifts me up to Thee.

Hope

Part 1 of 5

Through these biblical and ancient Christian prayers offer your adoration and gratitude to God, confess your sins, and ask for help to read his word and live the Christian life. If it helps, pray aloud and with physical gestures, such as raising your hands (1 Tim. 2:8) when you praise God's holy name or kneeling (Dan. 6:10) or lying prostrate (Luke 5:8) when you confess your sins. Using different postures to pray can engage your body and mind in new ways! "Stand up and bless the LORD your God from everlasting to everlasting" (Neh. 9:5).

Gloria Patri
Pray the Gloria Patri. Then take time to praise and thank God for specific blessings in your life.

Glory be to the Father, and to the Son, and to the Holy Ghost,
As it was in the beginning, is now, and ever shall be,
     world without end.
Amen.

Agnus Dei
Pray the Agnus Dei. Then take time to ask God through Jesus to forgive specific sins. Also offer prayers of lament. Pray that God would deal with sufferings and injustices both now and when Christ returns. Cry out, "O Sovereign

Lord, holy and true, how long before you will judge and avenge our blood on those who dwell on the earth?" (Rev. 6:10), or "Out of the depths I cry to you, O LORD! O Lord, hear my voice! Let your ears be attentive to the voice of my pleas for mercy!" (Ps. 130:1–2).

Lamb of God, who takes away the sins of the world,
    have mercy on us.
Lamb of God, who takes away the sins of the world,
    have mercy on us.
Lamb of God, who takes away the sins of the world,
    grant us peace. Amen.

The Lord's Prayer
Pray each line slowly. As you think about each petition, add your own specific requests.

Our Father in heaven,
hallowed be your name.
Your kingdom come,
your will be done,
    on earth as it is in heaven.
Give us this day our daily bread,
and forgive us our debts,
    as we also have forgiven our debtors.
And lead us not into temptation,
    but deliver us from evil.   Matthew 6:9–13

Prayer of Illumination
Almighty and immanent God, you have written in your word that the "blessed man" is the person who does not listen to the "counsel of the wicked"—the so-called wisdom of the world—but whose "delight" is in your law, and on your written revelation "he meditates day and night" (Ps 1:1, 2). Lord, help me to love your law, know your law, and live out your law. And, as I soak my

soul in your words day after day, make me "like a tree planted by streams of water that yields its fruit" year after year (1:3). Amen.

◆ ◆ ◆

Scripture Reading

Remember my affliction and my wanderings,
    the wormwood and the gall!
My soul continually remembers it
    and is bowed down within me.
But this I call to mind,
    and therefore I have hope:

The steadfast love of the LORD never ceases;
    his mercies never come to an end;
    they are new every morning;
    great is your faithfulness.
"The Lord is my portion," says my soul,
    "therefore I will hope in him." *Lamentations 3:19–24*

Concise Commentary

In the Hebrew Bible Lamentations is called 'Ekah, the Hebrew word for "how." This word is the first word of chapters 1, 2, and 3, and it is a good title because it underlines *how* much God's people in Jerusalem have suffered after the destruction of Jerusalem and during the exile. Because Lamentations comes right after the book of Jeremiah in our English Bibles and, like Jeremiah, describes the results of Babylon's siege in vivid detail, some people think Jeremiah wrote it. But, if so, he forgot to tell us! Whoever wrote this great piece of literature was a master writer, for he presents five interconnected and very carefully crafted poems (the first four poems are acrostics) that together depict a journey from devasting loss and personal shame to renewed hope and prayer for restoration. An acrostic poem is a poem that starts each verse (or, in the case of chapter 3, each three verses!) with a letter from the alphabet (A to Z in English; *aleph* to *tav* in Hebrew), a structure designed to offer full expression of the sorrows, confusion, and protest of God's people.

But Lamentations is more than a brilliant poem or group of poems; it is a sad song, or group of sad songs (laments). If you think of the book of Jeremiah as a kind of *scrapbook* of the prophet Jeremiah's emotions and thoughts of his own suffering soul as he witnesses God's judgment on Judah, then it is best to think of the book of Lamentations as a *songbook* for God's people who are expressing sadness, confessing sins, asking for forgiveness, seeking a newly restored relationship with God, expressing hope, and declaring total dependence on our faithful God. That said, at the center of this sad song the writer hits a few happy high notes, none higher than the note found in 3:19–24, which includes these beautiful lines about God's consistent and persistent mercy and his covenant faithfulness: "The steadfast love of the LORD never ceases; his mercies never come to an end; they are new every morning; great is your faithfulness." Here the poet expresses his hope that God will be consistent—just as he promised to bring justice upon evil and has done so, he will also fulfill his promise that mercy will triumph over justice; that is, he finds the judgment upon God's people to be the seedbed of hope that soon, in the near future, God will offer mercy to those who cling to him for restoration ("Restore us to yourself, O Lord, that we may be restored!," 5:21).

Prayer Prompt

Take time to praise God as king, declaring, "O Lord," you "reign forever," and "your throne endures to all generations," and thank him that he has not remained "exceedingly angry" at our sins or "utterly rejected us" for our iniquities but has shown us his absolute and everlasting mercies in Jesus. Praise him for the restoration now and forever, the new mercies that are ours now and will be ours when he makes "all things new."   *Based on Lamentations 5:19, 22; Revelation 21:5*

Memory Verse
"The Lord is my portion," says my soul; "therefore I will hope in him."   *Lamentations 3:24*

◆ ◆ ◆

"Great Is Thy Faithfulness"
Thomas O. Chisholm · 1923

Great is Thy faithfulness, O God my Father;
there is no shadow of turning with Thee;
Thou changest not, Thy compassions, they fail not;
as Thou hast been, Thou forever wilt be.

REFRAIN
Great is Thy faithfulness!
Great is Thy faithfulness!
Morning by morning new mercies I see;
all I have needed Thy hand hath provided:
great is Thy faithfulness, Lord, unto me!

Summer and winter, and springtime and harvest;
sun, moon, and stars in their courses above
join with all nature in manifold witness
to Thy great faithfulness, mercy, and love.

REFRAIN

Pardon for sin and a peace that endureth,
Thine own dear presence to cheer and to guide;
strength for today and bright hope for tomorrow:
blessings all mine, with ten thousand beside!

REFRAIN

Hope

Part 2 of 5

Adoration

Pray the prayer below. Then pause to praise God for who he is and what he has done.

My heart exults in the Lord;
There is none holy like the Lord:
    for there is none besides you;
The Lord kills and brings to life;
    he brings down to Sheol and raises up.
The Lord makes poor and makes rich;
    he brings low and he exalts.
He raises up the poor from the dust;
    he lifts the needy from the ash heap
to make them sit with princes
    and inherit a seat of honor.
For the pillars of the earth are the Lord's,
    and on them he has set the world.
The Lord will judge the ends of the earth;
    he will give strength to his king
    and exalt the horn of his anointed.   *1 Samuel 2:1, 2, 6–8, 10*

Confession
Pray the prayer below. Then take time to ask God through Jesus to forgive specific sins.

Almighty and eternal God and Father, I confess and acknowledge that I was conceived and born in sin and am therefore inclined to all evil and slow to do all good; that I transgress your holy commandments without ceasing and evermore corrupt myself. But I am very sorry for the same, and I pray your grace for help. Because of this, have mercy upon me, most gracious and merciful God and Father, through your Son the Lord Jesus Christ. Grant to me, and increase in me, your Holy Spirit, that I may recognize my sin and unrighteousness from the bottom of my heart, attain true repentance and sorrow for them, die to them wholly, and please you entirely by a new and godly life. Amen.
Strasbourg Liturgy (1545)

Thanksgiving
Thank God for the truth that "If we confess our sins, he is faithful and just to forgive us our sins and to cleanse us from all unrighteousness" (1 John 1:9), then pray the prayer below. Finally, take time to thank God for specific blessings in your life. Also feel free to offer Psalm 118:1 ("Oh give thanks to the Lord, *for he is good; for his steadfast love endures forever!") as a repeated refrain as you list off (and lift up!) to God people, events, gifts, and circumstances for which you are thankful.*

Grant me to live a life of gratitude to you for your innumerable benefits, O Lord my God! Instruct my ignorance and enlighten my darkness. You are my King, so take the entire possession of all my powers and faculties and let me be no longer under the dominion of sin. Give me a sincere and hearty repentance for all my grievous offenses and strengthen by your grace my resolutions on amendment and circumspection for the time to come.

Grant me also the spirit of prayer and supplication according to your own most gracious promises. Amen.   *Phillis Wheatley*

Supplication
After you pray the prayer below, feel free to add your own specific requests.

Lord God Almighty, I come before you today and ask that you would enable me to pass all the time of my pilgrimage here on earth in such a way that, when I pass from this world, I may be prepared to meet you in your heavenly kingdom. When I think of this life and its various temptations, when I look around and see the wickedness of the world and then contemplate also the weakness and corruption of my own nature, I recognize how easy it would be to fall under the power of such temptation. But I praise you, O Lord, for that abundant grace that is treasured up for me in Christ Jesus. I thank you for all the promises and encouragements given to me in your gospel, which is "the power of God for salvation to everyone who believes" (Rom 1:16). So I exalt you, because your Son has died as a sacrifice for sin and the Spirit of Christ has been given to sanctify me. And so I pray now for the filling of that same Spirit; I ask that you would fill me with the Holy Spirit so that in all I think and say and do this world might also be filled with the righteousness of God—that I may do your will, O Heavenly Father. Prepare me, I ask you, for every task of this day; arm me for every trial that may come upon me. Sanctify me, O Lord, in body, soul, and spirit. Help me this day to devote myself more fully to you; and may I, by your grace, be found walking in the fear of the Lord, fulfilling my vocation with Christian humility and simplicity. Amen.   *Henry Thornton*

Prayer of Illumination
O Lord, most merciful Father, receive your fugitive; to you I feel I must return. I knock; may your door be opened to me. Teach me the way to you. Amen.   *Augustine of Hippo*

＊ ＊ ＊

Scripture Reading

Now, therefore, thus you shall say to my servant David, "Thus says the LORD of hosts, I took you from the pasture, from following the sheep, that you should be prince over my people Israel. And I have been with you wherever you went and have cut off all your enemies from before you. And I will make for you a great name, like the name of the great ones of the earth. And I will appoint a place for my people Israel and will plant them, so that they may dwell in their own place and be disturbed no more. And violent men shall afflict them no more, as formerly, from the time that I appointed judges over my people Israel. And I will give you rest from all your enemies. Moreover, the LORD declares to you that the LORD will make you a house. When your days are fulfilled and you lie down with your fathers, I will raise up your offspring after you, who shall come from your body, and I will establish his kingdom. He shall build a house for my name, and I will establish the throne of his kingdom forever. I will be to him a father, and he shall be to me a son. When he commits iniquity, I will discipline him with the rod of men, with the stripes of the sons of men, but my steadfast love will not depart from him, as I took it from Saul, whom I put away from before you. And your house and your kingdom shall be made sure forever before me. Your throne shall be established forever." 2 Samuel 7:8–16

Concise Commentary

Two of the most significant promises in the Bible are the Abrahamic covenant in Genesis 12:1–3 (that God would make of Abraham "a great nation" and that through his offspring "all the families of the earth shall be blessed") and the Davidic covenant in 2 Samuel 7. Those two promises are given to two important men in Israel's history (Abraham and David), but it is clear that God is the one who assures that his promises will be fulfilled (notice the verb "I will" used eight times above)—and fulfilled in Jesus. We know this from the first verse of the New Testament ("Jesus Christ, the son of David, the son of Abraham," Matt. 1:1)! In fact, Matthew repeatedly emphasizes that Jesus is the promised king from David's line. In Matthew 12:23 the crowd asks, "Can this be the Son of David?" Then that question is answered in faith by three unlikely candidates: children crying out in the temple, "Hosanna to the Son of David!" (21:15); a Canaanite woman asking, "Have mercy on me, Lord, Son of David" (15:22); and two sets of two blind men who share in her chorus, "Have mercy on us, Son of David" (9:27; 20:30, 31). Moreover, a final and climactic time we hear the term "Son of David" comes in Jesus's dialogue with the Pharisees in Matthew 22, where he silences them by claiming that he is not only "the son of David" but David's Lord—the Lord God! Jesus silences them *then*; but he does not silence us *now*. With those Jewish children, that Gentile woman, and these two blind men we should shout, "Jesus, you are the Son of David! You are the promised king, who came from David's line to rescue us from sin's rule and rule over us forever."[9]

Prayer Prompt
Take time to ask God, through his Spirit, to broaden your understanding of how the promises of the Bible and the person and work of Jesus fit together. Thank him that all the stories of the Bible weave together to show the beautiful story of salvation. Praise him for the hope you have that Jesus will soon return as the King of kings and Lord of lords and conquer once and for all time sin, sorrow, and Satan.

Memory Verse
"The Lord is my portion," says my soul, "therefore I will hope in him." *Lamentations 3:24*

◆ ◆ ◆

"What Child Is This?"
W. Chatterton Dix · 1865

What Child is this, who, laid to rest,
On Mary's lap is sleeping?
Whom angels greet with anthems sweet,
While shepherds watch are keeping?

REFRAIN
This, this is Christ, the King,
Whom shepherds guard and angels sing:
Haste, haste to bring Him laud,
The Babe, the Son of Mary!

Why lies He in such mean estate,
Where ox and ass are feeding?
Good Christian, fear: for sinners here
The silent Word is pleading.

REFRAIN

So bring Him incense, gold, and myrrh,
Come, peasant, king to own Him.
The King of kings salvation brings;
Let loving hearts enthrone Him.

REFRAIN

Hope
Part 3 of 5

Adoration
Pray the prayer below. Then pause to praise God for who he is and what he has done.

Almighty and everlasting God, I now enter into your sacred presence under a deep sense of my weakness and unworthiness and your unspeakable greatness, holiness, and majesty. I approach you, at the same time, as a God of goodness, grace, and mercy, for you have made yourself known to us in Jesus Christ your Son and have proclaimed pardon to every repenting sinner through faith in the sacrifice that Christ has offered on the cross for us. I desire to honor you for this strong and sure foundation of hope, and I would now address you in the full assurance of faith, renouncing all confidence in myself, rejoicing in him who has become the hope of all the ends of the world. I praise the Lamb who died for us, has risen again, and is now exalted at your right hand, where he ever lives to make intercession for us. Amen.   Henry Thornton

Confession
Pray the prayer below. Then take time to ask God through Jesus to forgive specific sins.

Heavenly Father, you have loved me with an everlasting love, but I have gone my own way and rejected your will for my life. I am sorry for my sins and turn away from them. For the sake of your Son who died for me, forgive me, cleanse me, and change me. By your Holy Spirit enable me to live for you and to please you in every way, for the glory of our Lord Jesus Christ. Amen.

Thanksgiving

Thank God for the truth that "If we confess our sins, he is faithful and just to forgive us our sins and to cleanse us from all unrighteousness" (1 John 1:9), then pray the prayer below. Finally, take time to thank God for specific blessings in your life. Also feel free to offer Psalm 118:1 ("Oh give thanks to the LORD, for he is good; for his steadfast love endures forever!") as a repeated refrain as you list off (and lift up!) to God people, events, gifts, and circumstances for which you are thankful.

Giver of all good things, you have made me and saved me. Thank you! You have freed me from the power of darkness and brought me into the kingdom of light, moved me from death to life, from discord to peace, from ignorance to wisdom, from lies to truth, from slavery to sin to victory over it. Thank you for such a great salvation, and thank you for the blessing of your ministering angels who protect me, your Spirit-inspired word that guides me, your church that sustains me, your sacraments that strengthen me, your discipline that reminds me of your love of me. Thank you for all your provisions that enable me to grow in grace. Amen.   *Valley of Vision*[10]

Supplication

After you pray the prayer below, feel free to add your own specific requests.

Father, as I pray now the words of your Son, I ask—for the sake of your glory and my blessedness—that you would help me to be poor in spirit, to mourn over my sins and the sins of the world, to be meek, to hunger and thirst for righteousness, to be merciful, to be pure in heart, and to endure persecution for righteousness' sake. Father, I also ask that you would encourage me, through your Holy Spirit, to be active in good works, making me, as part of your church, the salt of the earth and the light of the world, so that many might give you glory. Lord, make me quick to forgive my enemies and those who have trespassed against me, quick to serve those in need, and slow to murder through thought, word, or deed. Purify my mind of all wicked and adulterous thoughts, allowing me to be faithful both to you and to my loved ones. Finally, Lord, in these days when lies abound (where they are the norm, make me abnormal), enable me to speak the truth always. Amen.   *Based on Matthew 5*

Prayer of Illumination
O God Almighty, the Father of your Christ, your only begotten Son, would you give me a body undefiled, a heart pure, a mind watchful, an unerring knowledge, the influence of the Holy Ghost for the obtaining and assured enjoying the truth, as I read your word. I ask this through Jesus Christ, by whom is glory to you, in the Holy Spirit, for ever. Amen.   *Apostolic Constitutions*

• • •

Scripture Reading
    Oh that my words were written!
        Oh that they were inscribed in a book!
    Oh that with an iron pen and lead
        they were engraved in the rock forever!
    For I know that my Redeemer lives,
        and at the last he will stand upon the earth.
    And after my skin has been thus destroyed,
        yet in my flesh I shall see God,

whom I shall see for myself,
  and my eyes shall behold, and not another.
  My heart faints within me!   *Job 19:23–27*

Concise Commentary

These verses stand out not only for their theological depth but
also for their unusual tone. Job has sounded hopeless since
chapter 3. Even in 19:10 he described God's taking whatever deep
root of hope Job still had and pulling it "up like a tree." But now
a new seed of hope emerges. Light flashes across the stage of this
depressing drama. We can almost hear Job singing his solo from
the score of Handel's *Messiah*.[11] Job knows for certain ("I know")
that a Redeemer, his personal and living Redeemer ("that my
Redeemer lives"), will soon "stand upon the earth" and save him
on judgment day ("at the last," 19:25). He goes so far as to express
his belief, or at least his hope, in a resurrection. He speaks of
dying ("after my skin has been thus destroyed," 19:26a) and yet
somehow seeing God vindicate him ("yet in my flesh I shall
see God," 19:26b). A bodily resurrection! The thought of this
beatific vision ("God, whom I shall see . . . my eyes shall behold,"
19:26–27b) and beautiful vindication is too much for him to take
in ("My heart faints within me!" 19:27c). This future theophany
is the ground of his hope.

While Job was not thinking about Jesus's death and resurrection and the hope that Christians gain from those
redemptive events when he uttered 19:25–27, we should read
this ancient text in view of our Redeemer. We can and should
rejoice that we have a Redeemer, a mediator who both is fully
God (1 Tim. 2:5) and also has turned away the full wrath of God
upon sinners (Rom. 5:9). We should celebrate that we have been
redeemed by his blood (Eph. 1:7; Col. 1:20; Rev. 5:9) and have a
"living hope" (1 Pet. 1:3) of physical resurrection, final vindication, and our future glorification and beatific vision ("We know
that when he appears we shall be like him, because we shall

see him as he is," 1 John 3:2), all because Jesus has conquered the grave. We should sing Handel's great aria in the *Messiah*, in which Job 19:25–26 is juxtaposed with 1 Corinthians 15:20 ("But now is Christ risen from the dead, and become the firstfruits of them that slept," KJV).[12]

Prayer Prompt
Take time to praise God for the hope of the resurrection of the body. Thank him for the greater knowledge we have and ask him to make you all the more certain that our Redeemer has conquered the grave and will return soon to judge evil and vindicate his people.

Memory Verse
"The LORD is my portion," says my soul, "therefore I will hope in him." *Lamentations 3:24*

◆ ◆ ◆

"Christ the Lord Is Risen Today"
Charles Wesley • *1739*

Christ the Lord is ris'n today, Alleluia!
Sons of men and angels say, Alleluia!
Raise your joys and triumphs high, Alleluia!
Sing, ye heav'ns, and earth reply, Alleluia!

Love's redeeming work is done, Alleluia!
Fought the fight, the battle won, Alleluia!
Death in vain forbids him rise, Alleluia!
Christ has opened paradise, Alleluia!

Lives again our glorious King, Alleluia!
Where, O death, is now thy sting? Alleluia!
Once he died our souls to save, Alleluia!
Where's thy victory, O grave? Alleluia!

Soar we now where Christ has led, Alleluia!
Foll'wing our exalted Head, Alleluia!
Made like him, like him we rise, Alleluia!
Ours the cross, the grave, the skies, Alleluia!

Hope

Part 4 of 5

Adoration

Pray the prayer below. Then pause to praise God for who he is and what he has done.

Praise the LORD!
Praise the LORD from the heavens;
   praise him in the heights!
Praise him, all his angels;
   praise him, all his hosts!

Praise him, sun and moon,
   praise him, all you shining stars!
Praise him, you highest heavens,
   and you waters above the heavens!   Psalm 148:1–4

Lord, I join the angels in heaven, the heavenly lights—the sun, moon, and stars—and all creation in the highest heaven to lift up your holy name. To you—Father, Son, and Spirit—be all honor and glory and praise! Amen.

Confession

Pray the prayer below. Then take time to ask God through Jesus to forgive specific sins.

Almighty God, unto whom all things are open, I set myself before you. Where can I go from your Spirit? Where can I flee from your presence? If I ascend to heaven, you are there! If I make my bed with the dead, you are there! If I dwell in the deepest part of the sea, you are there! Darkness and light are alike to you. You observed me before I was born, and in your book all my days were written. There is nothing hidden from you. And I take great comfort in this—for you know me intimately and care for me deeply. Yet your loving knowledge also disquiets my soul. I can fool others (and I do), I can fool myself (and I do), but I cannot fool you! Your intimate knowledge of me demands honesty. You have seen my outward sins, which I now confess: my deceptions, lies, gossip, hurtful words, loveless actions, my "me-first" self-focus, my irritability, my anger. Hear my confession of these sins. I also confess my inner sins, the attitudes contrary to the fruit of the Spirit, my jealousies, hatreds, and malice. Hear my confession of these sins too, Lord. Amen.
Based on Psalm 139

Thanksgiving

Thank God for the truth that "If we confess our sins, he is faithful and just to forgive us our sins and to cleanse us from all unrighteousness" (1 John 1:9), then pray the prayer below. Finally, take time to thank God for specific blessings in your life. Also feel free to offer Psalm 118:1 ("Oh give thanks to the Lord, *for he is good; for his steadfast love endures forever!") as a repeated refrain as you list off (and lift up!) to God people, events, gifts, and circumstances for which you are thankful.*

I give thanks to the Lord, my rock, my fortress, and my deliverer. I will remember his mercy, for he is gracious and compassionate. Thank you, Lord, for calling me to faith in Christ, for putting your Spirit within me, for giving me the mind of Christ, for gathering me into your church. I thank you, Lord, for extending your grace to me, for calling me to a life of gratitude, for calling me to service in your kingdom. Thanks be to God! Amen.   *Worship Sourcebook*[13]

Supplication
After you pray the prayer below, feel free to add your own specific requests.

O Lord, take away that which is mine, which is all naught, and give me that which is yours, which is all good. You are called Christ; anoint me therefore with your Holy Spirit. You are called a physician; according therefore to your name, heal me. You are called the Son of the living God; according therefore to your power, deliver me from the devil, the world, the flesh. You are called the resurrection; lift me up therefore from the damnable state wherein I most miserably lie. You are called the life; quicken me up therefore out of this death, wherewith through sin I am most grievously detained. You are called the way; lead me therefore from the vanities of this world and from the filthy pleasures of the flesh unto heavenly and spiritual things. You are called the truth; suffer me not therefore to walk in the way of error but to tread the path of truth in all my doings. You are called the light; put away therefore from me the works of darkness, that I may walk as the child of light in all goodness, righteousness, and truth. You are called a Savior; save me therefore from my sins, according to your name. You are called Alpha and Omega, that is, both the beginning and the end of goodness; begin therefore a good life in me and finish the same unto the glory of your blessed name. Amen. *Thomas Becon*

Prayer of Illumination
Deal bountifully with your servant,
    that I may live and keep your word.
Open my eyes, that I may behold
    wondrous things out of your law.   *Psalm 119:17–18*

Scripture Reading

But we do not want you to be uninformed, brothers, about those who are asleep, that you may not grieve as others do who have no hope. For since we believe that Jesus died and rose again, even so, through Jesus, God will bring with him those who have fallen asleep. For this we declare to you by a word from the Lord, that we who are alive, who are left until the coming of the Lord, will not precede those who have fallen asleep. For the Lord himself will descend from heaven with a cry of command, with the voice of an archangel, and with the sound of the trumpet of God. And the dead in Christ will rise first. Then we who are alive, who are left, will be caught up together with them in the clouds to meet the Lord in the air, and so we will always be with the Lord. Therefore encourage one another with these words.   *1 Thessalonians 4:13–18*

Concise Commentary

Throughout Paul's letters the theme of hope is featured. For example Paul includes hope in the triad of key Christian virtues—faith, hope, and love (1 Cor. 13:13)—and he often uses the word to refer to the "hope of eternal life" (Titus 1:2; 3:7), which he also labels "our blessed hope" (2:13), "the hope laid up for [us] in heaven" (Col. 1:5), "the hope of glory" (1:27), "the hope of righteousness" (Gal. 5:5), a hope that will be met with "the appearing of the glory of our great God and Savior Jesus Christ" (Titus 2:13), and the hope of sharing in heaven "the riches of his glorious inheritance in the saints" (Eph. 1:18). On that day our bodies and souls will then be without sin and perfectly glorious! Paul exhorts us to "rejoice in" this "hope" (Rom. 12:12). He also in 1 Thessalonians 4:13–18 reminds us to "encourage one another" (4:18)—especially those grieving the loss of loved ones—with the hope of heaven. We should "not grieve as others [unbelievers] do who have no hope" (4:13), for the ground of our hope is solid. "Since we believe that Jesus died and rose again" (4:14), we can be certain that those who have died "in Christ" will "rise" with Christ (4:16). And, when Christ does return, he has promised to gather his people together to be with him always: "We will always be with the Lord" (4:17).

Prayer Prompt
Take time to ask God, through his Spirit, to thank God that, in Jesus, we have the answer to the question Job asks: "Where then is my hope?" Jesus is "our Savior and . . . our hope." Thus, "rejoice in hope"!   *Based on Job 17:15; 1 Timothy 1:1; Romans 12:12*

> Memory Verse
> "The LORD is my portion," says my soul, "therefore I will hope in him."   *Lamentations 3:24*

♦ ♦ ♦

"If Thou but Suffer God to Guide Thee"
Georg Neumark • *1641* | *trans. Catherine Winkworth* • *1855, 1863*

If thou but suffer God to guide thee,
and hope in him through all thy ways,
he'll give thee strength, whate'er betide thee,
and bear thee through the evil days.
Who trusts in God's unchanging love
build on the Rock that naught can move.

Only be still, and wait his leisure
in cheerful hope, with heart content
to take whate'er thy Father's pleasure

and all-discerning love hath sent;
nor doubt our inmost wants are known
to him who chose us for his own.

Sing, pray, and keep his ways unswerving,
so do thine own part faithfully,
and trust his word; though undeserving,
thou yet shalt find it true for thee;
God never yet forsook at need
the soul that trusted him indeed.

Hope

Part 5 of 5

Adoration
Pray the prayer below. Then pause to praise God for who he is and what he has done.

Praise the LORD!
Praise, O servants of the LORD,
     praise the name of the LORD!

Blessed be the name of the LORD
     from this time forth and forevermore!
From the rising of the sun to its setting,
     the name of the LORD is to be praised!   *Psalm 113:1–3*

Confession
Pray the prayer below. Then take time to ask God through Jesus to forgive specific sins.

Almighty God, Father of our Lord Jesus Christ, maker of all things, judge of all people, I acknowledge and confess the grievous sins and wickedness that I have so often committed by thought, word, and deed against your divine majesty, provoking most justly your anger and indignation against me. I earnestly repent and am deeply sorry for these wrongdoings; the memory of them weighs me down, and the burden of them is too great for me to bear. Have mercy upon me, most merciful Father; for your Son my Lord Jesus Christ's sake, forgive me all that is past; and grant that from this time onward I may always serve and please you in newness of life, to the honor and glory of your name, through Jesus Christ our Lord. Amen.

Thanksgiving

Thank God for the truth that "If we confess our sins, he is faithful and just to forgive us our sins and to cleanse us from all unrighteousness" (1 John 1:9), then pray the prayer below. Finally, take time to thank God for specific blessings in your life. Also feel free to offer Psalm 118:1 ("Oh give thanks to the LORD, for he is good; for his steadfast love endures forever!") as a repeated refrain as you list off (and lift up!) to God people, events, gifts, and circumstances for which you are thankful.

Praise and thanksgiving be unto you, O God, who brought again from the dead our Lord Jesus Christ and set him at your right hand in the kingdom of glory. Praise and thanksgiving be unto you, O Lord Jesus Christ, you Lamb of God who has redeemed us by your blood, you heavenly priest who ever lives to make intercession for us, you eternal King who comes again to make all things new. Praise and thanksgiving be unto you, O Holy Spirit, who has shed abroad the love of God, who makes us alive together with Christ, and who makes us to sit with him in heavenly places and to taste the good word of God and the powers of the age to come. Blessing and glory, and wisdom and thanksgiving and honor and power and might, be unto you our God forever and ever. Amen.   *Thomas F. Torrance*

Supplication
After you pray the prayer below, feel free to add your own specific requests.

How long will you judge unjustly
    and show partiality to the wicked?

Give justice to the weak and the fatherless;
  maintain the right of the afflicted and the destitute.
Rescue the weak and the needy;
  deliver them from the hand of the wicked.

Arise, O God, judge the earth;
  for you shall inherit all the nations!   Psalm 82:2–4, 8

Prayer of Illumination
Lord, I am now entering into your presence, to hear you speak from heaven to me, to receive your rain and spiritual dew, which never return in vain but ripen a harvest of either corn or weeds, of grace or judgment. My heart is prepared, O Lord, my heart is prepared to learn and to love any of your words. Your law is my counselor; I will be ruled by it. It is my physician; I will be patient under it. It is my schoolmaster; I will be obedient to it. Amen.   Edward Reynolds

• • •

Scripture Reading
Then I saw a new heaven and a new earth, for the first heaven and the first earth had passed away, and the sea was no more. And I saw the holy city, new Jerusalem, coming down out of heaven from God, prepared as a bride adorned for her husband. And I heard a loud voice from the throne saying, "Behold, the dwelling place of God is with man. He will dwell with them, and they will be his people, and God himself will be with them as their God. He will wipe away every tear from their eyes, and death shall be no more, neither shall there be mourning, nor crying, nor pain anymore, for the former things have passed away."

And he who was seated on the throne said, "Behold, I am making all things new." Also he said, "Write this down, for these words are trustworthy and true." And he said to me, "It is done!

I am the Alpha and the Omega, the beginning and the end. To the thirsty I will give from the spring of the water of life without payment. The one who conquers will have this heritage, and I will be his God and he will be my son. But as for the cowardly, the faithless, the detestable, as for murderers, the sexually immoral, sorcerers, idolaters, and all liars, their portion will be in the lake that burns with fire and sulfur, which is the second death."
Revelation 21:1–8

Concise Commentary

Throughout the ages and in every country around the world Christians have made this simple confession of faith: "Christ has died; Christ is risen; Christ will come again." We could add to that, "Christ came to earth; Christ was born; Christ lived the perfect life." We can think of the Son of God's mission on earth as summarized in those six key events: (1) He came from heaven to earth. (2) He was born of Mary in the town of Bethlehem. (3) He lived a life without sin, healed the sick, cast out demons, taught truths, and welcomed people to follow him. (4) He suffered and died on the cross on behalf of sinners. (5) He rose in glory from the grave and ascended into heaven. (6) Someday soon he will come again to gather his people, judge evil, and renew creation. As believers, we should long for the day when Christ returns and the promise is fulfilled of the new Jerusalem, where there will be no sinners who hate God (and no sin in us who have sought to love God), no death, and no sorrow. On that day, in our beautiful and glorious new home, we will have access to God, will experience complete satisfaction, and together with God's people from every nation "will worship" and "reign forever and ever" (Rev. 22:3, 5) with our great God.

Prayer Prompt

Take time to ask God, through his Spirit, to help you long for the return of Christ—to cry out today and every day until his return,

"Come, Lord Jesus!" (Rev. 22:20). And pray that the Lord of the harvest would give you more passion, urgency, and opportunity to share the gospel with lost people who need to hear the offer of God's salvation from sin, death, and hell.

> Memory Verse
> "The LORD is my portion," says my soul, "therefore I will hope in him." *Lamentations 3:24*

• • •

"The King Shall Come When Morning Dawns"
Jon Brownlie • 1907

The King shall come when morning dawns
and light triumphant breaks,
when beauty gilds the eastern hills
and life to joy awakes.

Not as of old a little child,
to bear, and fight, and die,
but crowned with glory like the sun
that lights the morning sky.

O brighter than the rising morn
when He, victorious, rose
and left the lonesome place of death,
despite the rage of foes.

O brighter than that glorious morn
shall this fair morning be,

when Christ, our King, in beauty comes,
and we His face shall see.

The King shall come when morning dawns,
and light and beauty brings;
"Hail, Christ the Lord!" Thy people pray,
come quickly, King of kings!

Wisdom

Part 1 of 5

Through these biblical and ancient Christian prayers offer your adoration and gratitude to God, confess your sins, and ask for help to read his word and live the Christian life. If it helps, pray aloud and with physical gestures, such as raising your hands (1 Tim. 2:8) when you praise God's holy name or kneeling (Dan. 6:10) or lying prostrate (Luke 5:8) when you confess your sins. Using different postures to pray can engage your body and mind in new ways! "Stand up and bless the LORD your God from everlasting to everlasting" (Neh. 9:5).

Gloria Patri
Pray the Gloria Patri. Then take time to praise and thank God for specific blessings in your life.

Glory be to the Father, and to the Son, and to the Holy Ghost,
As it was in the beginning, is now, and ever shall be,
    world without end.
Amen.

Agnus Dei
Pray the Agnus Dei. Then take time to ask God through Jesus to forgive specific sins. Also offer prayers of lament. Pray that God would deal with

sufferings and injustices both now and when Christ returns. Cry out, "O Sovereign Lord, holy and true, how long before you will judge and avenge our blood on those who dwell on the earth?" (Rev. 6:10), or "Out of the depths I cry to you, O Lord! O Lord, hear my voice! Let your ears be attentive to the voice of my pleas for mercy!" (Ps. 130:1–2).

Lamb of God, who takes away the sins of the world,
    have mercy on us.
Lamb of God, who takes away the sins of the world,
    have mercy on us.
Lamb of God, who takes away the sins of the world,
    grant us peace. Amen.

The Lord's Prayer
Pray each line slowly. As you think about each petition, add your own specific requests.

Our Father in heaven,
hallowed be your name.
Your kingdom come,
your will be done,
    on earth as it is in heaven.
Give us this day our daily bread,
and forgive us our debts,
    as we also have forgiven our debtors.
And lead us not into temptation,
    but deliver us from evil.   *Matthew 6:9–13*

Prayer of Illumination
Almighty God, Father of our Lord Jesus Christ, establish and confirm me in your truth by your Holy Spirit. Reveal to me what I do not know; perfect in me what is lacking; strengthen me in what I know; and keep me faithful in your service; through Jesus Christ my Lord. Amen.   *Clement of Rome*

• • •

Scripture Reading

Solomon loved the LORD, walking in the statutes of David his father, only he sacrificed and made offerings at the high places. And the king went to Gibeon to sacrifice there, for that was the great high place. Solomon used to offer a thousand burnt offerings on that altar. At Gibeon the LORD appeared to Solomon in a dream by night, and God said, "Ask what I shall give you." And Solomon said, "You have shown great and steadfast love to your servant David my father, because he walked before you in faithfulness, in righteousness, and in uprightness of heart toward you. And you have kept for him this great and steadfast love and have given him a son to sit on his throne this day. And now, O LORD my God, you have made your servant king in place of David my father, although I am but a little child. I do not know how to go out or come in. And your servant is in the midst of your people whom you have chosen, a great people, too many to be numbered or counted for multitude. Give your servant therefore an understanding mind to govern your people, that I may discern between good and evil, for who is able to govern this your great people?"

It pleased the Lord that Solomon had asked this. And God said to him, "Because you have asked this, and have not asked for yourself long life or riches or the life of your enemies, but have asked for yourself understanding to discern what is right, behold, I now do according to your word. Behold, I give you a wise and discerning mind, so that none like you has been before you and none like you shall arise after you. I give you also what you have not asked, both riches and honor, so that no other king shall compare with you, all your days. And if you will walk in my ways, keeping my statutes and my commandments, as your father David walked, then I will lengthen your days."

And Solomon awoke, and behold, it was a dream.   1 Kings 3:3–15

That which had been a dream for Solomon—also named Jedidiah (which means "beloved of the LORD"; 2 Sam. 12:25)—became a reality. God bestowed upon him his wish for wisdom, along with what he did not ask for: "both riches and honor" (1 Kings 4:12). Solomon was so rich that he sat upon "a great ivory throne and overlaid it with the finest gold" (10:18) and drank from "vessels of gold" (10:21), and he was so honored that "people of all nations came to hear the wisdom of Solomon" (4:34), including royal dignitaries such as the Queen of Sheba. Upon her visit, when "she came to test him with hard questions" (10:1), she learned firsthand of his measureless mind: "And Solomon answered all her questions; there was nothing hidden from the king that he could not explain to her" (10:3). She was so astonished that "there was no more breath in her" (10:5). However, Solomon's vast wisdom had its limits, and his seemingly indestructible kingdom had cracks in its foundation. Even though "God gave Solomon wisdom and understanding beyond measure, and breadth of mind like the sand of the seashore" (4:29), sin got the best of him. Israel's king was to have only one wife, someone from the tribes of Israel, but King Solomon "had 700 wives, who were princesses, and 300 concubines" (11:3) from among the pagan nations, who turned his heart away from loving Yahweh and toward loving foreign gods. Mere idols! Such idolatry was his downfall, and with it the weakening and severing of his kingdom after his death.

Of course, and obviously, Solomon was not the ultimate promised king of 2 Samuel 7 (see Day 17) who would rule over God's forever kingdom. But Jesus is, and he tells us as much. As he boldly announces to the scribes and the Pharisees, "The queen of the South will rise up at the judgment with this generation and condemn it, for she came from the ends of the earth to hear the wisdom of Solomon, and behold, something greater than Solomon is here" (Matt. 12:42). Jesus, who is God's "beloved Son," with whom he was "well pleased" from the day of his birth to his ascension (3:17), is greater than Solomon in "power and wealth and wisdom and might and honor and glory and blessing" (Rev. 5:12; cf. Phil. 2:9–11; 1 Tim. 1:17; Heb. 2:7). He "is the blessed and only Sovereign, the King of kings and Lord of lords" (1 Tim. 6:15; cf. Rev. 17:14; 19:16), who "shall reign forever and ever" over God's kingdom (Rev. 11:15). And from the cradle to the cross he walked the road of wisdom each step of the way. "Denying himself the usual rewards of righteousness—long life, a good reputation, a strong marriage, healthy children, material prosperity—he submitted to the wise will of his Father, enduring the crown of thorns, a humiliating death, and spiritual abandonment so that in his sufferings he might atone for our sins and demonstrate the very wisdom and power of God."[14] What a King! What a Savior!

Prayer Prompt
Take time to ask God, through his Spirit, to give you the wisdom and understanding both to acknowledge Jesus as your King and Savior and to live in accord with his ways all your days. Also, as we are all prone to wander from the path of wisdom as Solomon did, ask that God would keep you on the straight and narrow road that leads to eternal life.

Memory Verse
If any of you lacks wisdom, let him ask God, who gives generously to all without reproach, and it will be given him. (James 1:5)

◆ ◆ ◆

"Come, Thou Fount"
Robert Robinson · 1758 | altered Martin Madan · 1760

Come, thou Fount of every blessing;
tune my heart to sing thy grace;
streams of mercy, never ceasing,
call for songs of loudest praise.
Teach me some melodious sonnet,
sung by flaming tongues above;
praise the mount! I'm fixed upon it,
mount of God's unchanging love!

Here I raise my Ebenezer;
hither by thy help I'm come;
and I hope, by thy good pleasure,
safely to arrive at home.
Jesus sought me when a stranger,
wand'ring from the fold of God;
he, to rescue me from danger,
interposed his precious blood.

O to grace how great a debtor
daily I'm constrained to be!
Let that grace now, like a fetter,
bind my wand'ring heart to thee.
Prone to wander, Lord, I feel it,
prone to leave the God I love;
here's my heart; O take and seal it;
seal it for thy courts above.

Wisdom

Part 2 of 5

Adoration
Pray the prayer below. Then pause to praise God for who he is and what he has done.

Oh, the depth of the riches and wisdom and knowledge of God! How unsearchable are his judgments and how inscrutable his ways!

"For who has known the mind of the Lord,
 or who has been his counselor?"
"Or who has given a gift to him
 that he might be repaid?"

For from him and through him and to him are all things. To him be glory forever. Amen.   Romans 11:33–36

Confession
Pray the prayer below. Then take time to ask God through Jesus to forgive specific sins.

Gracious God, I acknowledge that I am a sinner and that I have sinned. My mind and heart have wandered from the way of life, from steadfast obedience to your righteous word. So I come to you now, confessing my sins and asking you, through the holy blood of Jesus Christ, to forgive me and cleanse me from all iniquities. Lord, I also ask that you would purify my soul of the acts of my sinful nature and fill me with your Spirit. Conquer my sin and generously bestow upon me the fruit of the Spirit: love, joy, peace, patience, kindness, goodness, faithfulness, gentleness, and self-control. Amen.   Based on Psalm 118

Thanksgiving

Thank God for the truth that "If we confess our sins, he is faithful and just to forgive us our sins and to cleanse us from all unrighteousness" (1 John 1:9), then pray the prayer below. Finally, take time to thank God for specific blessings in your life. Also feel free to offer Psalm 118:1 ("Oh give thanks to the LORD, for he is good; for his steadfast love endures forever!") as a repeated refrain as you list off (and lift up!) to God people, events, gifts, and circumstances for which you are thankful.

Let the redeemed of the LORD say so,
    whom he has redeemed from trouble
Let them thank the LORD for his steadfast love,
    for his wondrous works to the children of man!
And let them offer sacrifices of thanksgiving,
    and tell of his deeds in songs of joy!
Let them thank the LORD for his steadfast love,
    for his wondrous works to the children of man!
    Psalm 107:2, 8, 22, 31

Supplication

After you pray the prayer below, feel free to add your own specific requests.

Grant, O Lord, that from this hour, I may know only that which is worthy to be known; that I may love only that which is truly lovely; that I may praise only that which chiefly pleases you; and that I may esteem what you esteem and despise that which is contemptible in your sight! Suffer me no longer to judge by imperfect perception either of my own senses, or the senses of men ignorant like myself. But enable me to judge both of visible and invisible things, by the Spirit of truth. And, above all, to know and to obey your will. Amen.   *Thomas à Kempis*

Prayer of Illumination
Help me by your Spirit; let your fear be upon me; let your word come unto me in power, and be received in love, with an attentive, reverent, and obedient mind. Make it to me the savor of life unto life. Amen.   *Richard Baxter*

◆ ◆ ◆

Scripture Reading
The proverbs of Solomon, son of David, king of Israel:

To know wisdom and instruction,
     to understand words of insight,
to receive instruction in wise dealing,
     in righteousness, justice, and equity;
to give prudence to the simple,
     knowledge and discretion to the youth—
Let the wise hear and increase in learning,
     and the one who understands obtain guidance,
to understand a proverb and a saying,
     the words of the wise and their riddles.

The fear of the LORD is the beginning of knowledge;
     fools despise wisdom and instruction.   *Proverbs 1:1–7*

Concise Commentary
Wisdom can involve both knowledge and skill. In exile "God gave" Daniel and his three friends "learning and skill in all

literature" (Dan. 1:17). Similarly, the Lord gave "every craftsman . . . skill and intelligence to know how to do any work in the construction of the sanctuary [the tabernacle] . . . in accordance with all that the LORD has commanded." (Ex. 36:1). However, according to the Wisdom Literature of the Bible (e.g., Proverbs, Ecclesiastes, and Job), wisdom is more than the acquisition of information or the skill to build an elaborate edifice. Biblical wisdom is understanding how the world works and how God wants us to live in it. Moreover, it is obtained not through natural intelligence, an elite education, or years of training and experience but through fearing God: "The fear of the LORD [Yahweh] is the beginning of knowledge" (Prov. 1:7; cf. 9:10; 15:33). So the Bible's wisdom literature is not God's version of Ben Franklin's *Poor Richard's Almanack*—"Early to bed and early to rise, makes a man healthy, wealthy, and wise"—or the ancient Chinese sayings of Confucius—"Silence is a friend who will never betray." What distinguishes the content of biblical wisdom from the rest of the world's wisdom literature are declarations like the ones found at the beginning of Proverbs (1:7), the end of Ecclesiastes (12:13), and the climatic midpoint of Job (28:28). True wisdom is acquired only through a proper relationship with Yahweh, coupled with a fitting attitude and actions toward him. And here at the start of Proverbs Solomon calls everyone who needs God's wisdom—the young, the simple, and those already wise—to listen up so as to receive *practical* wisdom ("instruction in wise dealing" and "prudence . . . knowledge and discretion," Prov. 1:3–4), *intellectual* wisdom (understanding of insightful words, 1:2b, 4b), *moral* wisdom ("instruction . . . in righteousness, justice, and equity," 1:3b), and even *mysterious* wisdom ("guidance" and the ability to comprehend "the words of the wise and their riddles," 1:5–6).[15]

Prayer Prompt
Take time to ask God, through his Spirit, to help you understand and believe with all your heart, mind, and strength that

"the fear of the LORD is clean, enduring forever" and that "the rules of the LORD are true, and righteous altogether" (Ps. 19:9). Also, ask this day for your daily dose of wisdom! Trusting that "the LORD gives wisdom" (Prov. 2:6) and loves to give wisdom, "get wisdom" (4:5)—wisdom that will protect, guide, and enlighten.

Memory Verse

If any of you lacks wisdom, let him ask God, who gives generously to all without reproach, and it will be given him.   *James 1:5*

◆ ◆ ◆

"Be Thou My Vision"
trans. Mary E. Byrne ◆ 1905

Be Thou my vision, O Lord of my heart;
naught be all else to me, save that Thou art;
Thou my best thought, by day or by night,
waking or sleeping, Thy presence my light.

Be Thou my wisdom, and Thou my true word;
I ever with Thee and Thou with me, Lord;
Thou my great Father, I Thy true son;
Thou in me dwelling, and I with Thee one.

Riches I heed not, nor man's empty praise,
Thou mine inheritance, now and always:
Thou and Thou only, first in my heart,
High King of Heaven, my treasure Thou art.

High King of heaven, Thou heaven's bright Sun,
grant me its joys after vict'ry is won;
Heart of my own heart, whatever befall,
still be Thou my Vision, O Ruler of all.

Wisdom

Part 3 of 5

Adoration

Pray the prayer below. Then pause to praise God for who he is and what he has done.

Your understanding, O Lord, is infinite, for you tell the number of the stars and call them all by their names. You are wonderful in counsel, excellent in working, wise in heart, and mighty in strength. O Lord, how manifold are your works; in wisdom you have made them all, according to the counsel of your own will. Oh the depth of your wisdom and knowledge! How unsearchable are your judgments, and your ways beyond finding out! The heavens, even the heavens, are yours, and all the hosts of them. The earth is yours, and the fullness thereof. The world, and all they that dwell therein. In your hand are the deep places of the earth, and the strength of the hills is yours also. The sea is yours, for you made it, and your hands formed the dry land. All the beasts of the forest are yours, and the cattle upon a thousand hills. You are therefore a great God and a great King. Amen.
Matthew Henry

Confession

Pray the prayer below. Then take time to ask God through Jesus to forgive specific sins.

Lord, you spoke through your prophet Joel and offered your people then what you offer me today. "Yet even now," declares the LORD, "return to me with all your heart, with fasting, with weeping, and with mourning; and rend your hearts and not your garments." Help me, to return to you my Lord God, for I know and believe that you "are gracious and merciful, slow to anger, and abounding in steadfast love." Amen.   *Based on Joel 2:12–13*

Thanksgiving
Thank God for the truth that "If we confess our sins, he is faithful and just to forgive us our sins and to cleanse us from all unrighteousness" (1 John 1:9), then pray the prayer below. Finally, take time to thank God for specific blessings in your life. Also feel free to offer Psalm 118:1 ("Oh give thanks to the LORD, for he is good; for his steadfast love endures forever!") as a repeated refrain as you list off (and lift up!) to God people, events, gifts, and circumstances for which you are thankful.

Blessed be the name of God forever and ever,
    to whom belong wisdom and might.
He changes times and seasons;
    he removes kings and sets up kings;
he gives wisdom to the wise
    and knowledge to those who have understanding;
he reveals deep and hidden things;
    he knows what is in the darkness,
    and the light dwells with him.
To you, O God of my fathers,
    I give thanks and praise,
for you have given me wisdom and might.   *Daniel 2:20–23a*

Supplication
After you pray the prayer below, feel free to add your own specific requests.

Almighty God, in whom we live and move and have our being, you have made us for yourself, so that our hearts are restless until they rest in you. Grant me today, Lord, purity of heart and strength of purpose, so that no selfish passion may hinder me from knowing your will, no weakness from doing it. Grant that in your light I may see clearly and in your service find my perfect freedom. I ask this through Christ, our Lord. Amen. *Augustine of Hippo*

Prayer of Illumination
Lord God, as I read and meditate on your word, may my love "abound more and more, with knowledge and all discernment, so that [I] may approve what is excellent, and so be pure and blameless for the day of Christ." Amen.   *Based on Phil. 1:9–10*

• • •

Scripture Reading
> From where, then, does wisdom come?
>> And where is the place of understanding?
> It is hidden from the eyes of all living
>> and concealed from the birds of the air.
> Abaddon and Death say,
>> "We have heard a rumor of it with our ears."
>
> God understands the way to it,
>> and he knows its place.
> For he looks to the ends of the earth
>> and sees everything under the heavens.
> When he gave to the wind its weight
>> and apportioned the waters by measure,
> when he made a decree for the rain
>> and a way for the lightning of the thunder,
> then he saw it and declared it;
>> he established it, and searched it out.
> And he said to man,

"Behold, the fear of the Lord, that is wisdom,
and to turn away from evil is understanding." *Job 28:20–28*

Concise Commentary

The beautiful poem in Job 28 is the literary, and perhaps the theological, climax of the book. Job (whom I take to be the speaker) begins by dwelling on human wisdom—an intelligence, ingenuity, and industry unsurpassed in all creation—through the illustration of our unique ability to mine precious stones, metals, and jewels from the earth. But before we boast, saying, "We are 'man'—watch us roar and soar, or at least explore," in the next stanza (28:12–22) we are put in our place. While we can probe the mysteries of our earthly domain, we cannot probe the mysteries of the heavenly domain. With resourcefulness and determination we can search the extremities of the earth's surface, but we cannot scratch the surface of wisdom. We can bring to light all hidden material things buried in the depths of the earth, but we cannot unearth Wisdom, the true light of the world. The best that this world can offer to aid humanity in its search for wisdom is merely a "rumor of it" (28:22). On, in, and above the earth, wisdom cannot be found by man's best efforts. With the living and with the dead, wisdom cannot be found. That is the message of the bookends of this middle section (28:12–14, 20–22). While man can extract precious metals from the earth, the acquisition of wisdom from the "land of the living" (28:13) is an impossibility.

However, all hope is not lost! After mining (pun intended) through twenty-two verses of this twenty-eight-verse poem, we are still left without an answer to the key question, "Where shall wisdom be found?" (28:12). Thankfully, in the third stanza (28:23–28) wisdom gives up the secret of its location. The solution to the search for wisdom is "God" (28:23) and the "fear of the Lord" (28:28). While human ingenuity cannot find wisdom and human wealth cannot buy wisdom, "God understands the way to it, and he knows its place" (28:23). God alone knows where wisdom is to be found, because he alone is omniscient ("He looks to the ends of the earth and sees everything under the heavens," 28:24). He also knows where wisdom ("it") is to be found; God ("he") used it to establish and govern the world. If you want wisdom, go to God. Go to God on your knees.[16]

Prayer Prompt
Take time to ask God, through his Spirit, to reveal to you through the reading of his word something of the "manifold wisdom of God" revealed or "realized" in our Lord Jesus Christ (see Eph. 3:8–11); to uncover "all the treasures of wisdom and knowledge" that are "hidden" in Christ (Col. 2:3), your Redeemer.

> Memory Verse
> If any of you lacks wisdom, let him ask God, who gives generously
> to all without reproach, and it will be given him. (James 1:5)

• • •

"Immortal, Invisible God Only Wise"
Walter C. Smith · *1867*

Immortal, invisible, God only wise,
in light inaccessible hid from our eyes,
most bless-ed, most glorious, the Ancient of Days,
almighty, victorious, thy great name we praise.

Unresting, unhasting, and silent as light,
nor wanting, nor wasting, thou rulest in might;

thy justice like mountains high soaring above
thy clouds, which are fountains of goodness and love.

To all life thou givest, to both great and small;
in all life thou livest, the true life of all;
we blossom and flourish as leaves on the tree,
and wither and perish but naught changeth thee.

Great Father of glory, pure Father of light,
thine angels adore thee, all veiling their sight;
all praise we would render, O help us to see
'tis only the splendor of light hideth thee.

Wisdom

Part 4 of 5

Adoration
Pray the prayer below. Then pause to praise God for who he is and what he has done..

Bless the LORD, O my soul!
    O LORD my God, you are very great!
You are clothed with splendor and majesty,
      covering yourself with light as with a garment,
      stretching out the heavens like a tent.

O LORD, how manifold are your works!
    In wisdom have you made them all;
      the earth is full of your creatures.   Psalm 104:1–2, 24

Confession
Pray the prayer below. Then take time to ask God through Jesus to forgive specific sins.

O Lord, have mercy upon me.
O Christ, have mercy upon me.
O Spirit, have mercy upon me.
O God the Father in heaven, I beg you, hear me.
O God the Son, Redeemer of the world, I beg you, hear me.
O God the Holy Spirit, our Comforter, I beg you, hear me.
Be gracious, good Lord.

Help me, good Lord.
Save me, good Lord,
from my sin and from all evil.
Good Lord, deliver me.
Lord, have mercy upon me. Amen.   *Gregory the Great*

Thanksgiving

Thank God for the truth that "If we confess our sins, he is faithful and just to forgive us our sins and to cleanse us from all unrighteousness" (1 John 1:9), then pray the prayer below. Finally, take time to thank God for specific blessings in your life. Also feel free to offer Psalm 118:1 ("Oh give thanks to the LORD, *for he is good; for his steadfast love endures forever!") as a repeated refrain as you list off (and lift up!) to God people, events, gifts, and circumstances for which you are thankful.*

Heavenly Father and Holy Spirit, how thankful I am for Jesus the Son, for in him is found every aspect of my salvation and sanctification. If I seek the gifts of the Spirit, they are found in his anointing; strength in his dominion; purity in his conception; gentleness in his birth; redemption in his passion; acquittal in his condemnation; remission of the curse in his cross; satisfaction in his sacrifice; purification in his blood; reconciliation in his descent into hell; mortification of the flesh in his tomb; newness of life and immortality in his resurrection; inheritance of the heavenly kingdom in his entrance into heaven; protection, security, and abundant supply of all blessings in his eternal reign and everlasting kingdom. Thank you, Father. Thank you, Son. Thank you, Spirit. Amen.   *John Calvin*

Supplication

After you pray the prayer below, feel free to add your own specific requests.

Lord, high and holy, meek and lowly, you have brought me to the valley of vision, where I live in the depths but see you in the heights; hemmed in by mountains of sin, I behold your glory. Let me learn by paradox that the way down is the way up, that to be low is to be high, that the broken heart is the healed heart, that the contrite spirit is the rejoicing spirit, that the repenting soul is the victorious soul, that to have nothing is to possess all, that to bear the cross is to wear the crown, that to give is to receive, that the valley is the place of vision. Lord, in the daytime stars can be seen from deepest wells, and the deeper the wells, the brighter your stars shine. Let me find your light in my darkness, your life in my death, your joy in my sorrow, your grace in my sin, your riches in my poverty, your glory in my valley. Amen. *Valley of Vision*[17]

Prayer of Illumination

Lord, I thank you that you have revealed yourself through creation: "The heavens declare the glory of God, and the sky above proclaims his handiwork. Day to day pours out speech, and night to night reveals knowledge." I also thank you that you have revealed yourself through your written revelation. As I read your perfect word, give me wisdom, enlighten my mind, revive my soul, make my heart rejoice, confront me with your warnings, and woo me with your rewards. Amen.   *Based on Psalm 19:1–2, 7–8, 11*

• • •

Scripture Reading

For the word of the cross is folly to those who are perishing, but to us who are being saved it is the power of God. For it is written, "I will destroy the wisdom of the wise, and the discernment of the discerning I will thwart." Where is the one who is wise? Where is the scribe? Where is the debater of this age? Has not God made foolish the wisdom of the world? For since, in the wisdom of God, the world did not know God through wisdom, it pleased God through the folly of what we preach to save those who believe. For Jews demand signs and Greeks seek wisdom, but we preach Christ crucified, a stumbling block to Jews and folly to Gentiles, but to those who are called, both Jews and Greeks, Christ the power of God and the wisdom of God. For the foolishness of God is wiser than men, and the weakness of God is stronger than men. For consider your calling, brothers: not many of you were wise according to worldly standards, not many were powerful, not many were of noble birth. But God chose what is foolish in the world to shame the wise; God chose what is weak in the world to shame the strong; God chose what is low and despised in the world, even things that are not, to bring to nothing things that are, so that no human being might boast in the presence of God. And because of him you are in Christ Jesus, who became to us wisdom from God, righteousness and sanctification and redemption, so that, as it is written, "Let the one who boasts, boast in the Lord." 1 Corinthians 1:18–31

Concise Commentary

While it is true that in creation and providence God manifests his wisdom, it is likewise true, as taught throughout the New Testament, that God most perfectly or more fully manifests his wisdom in the person and work of his Son, our Lord Jesus Christ. In his incarnation Jesus brought "wisdom from above" (James 3:17) down to earth. And such wisdom was demonstrated through his growth in wisdom, teaching of wisdom, and life of wisdom (his perfect, God-fearing, sin-renouncing life), but ultimately through his sacrificial death. The apostle Paul speaks in Ephesians 3:8–11 of the "manifold wisdom of God" revealed or "realized" in our Lord Jesus Christ; in Colossians 2:3 he explains how "all the treasures of wisdom and knowledge" are "hidden" in Christ; finally, in 1 Corinthians 1:18–24 he writes that the preaching of "Christ" and him "crucified" is the "wisdom of God." Those who trust that God through the crucifixion made Christ to be "wisdom from God, righteousness and sanctification and redemption" (1:30) appear foolish to the unwise—to the overly-wise-in-its-own-eyes—world. Yet we are no fools if we abandon human pride and power to find the "secret and hidden wisdom of God" (2:2) now revealed in "Christ and him crucified" (2:2). The apparent folly of a crucified God is God's wisdom most perfectly revealed. That is where wisdom is ultimately found.[18]

Prayer Prompt
Take time to ask God, through his Spirit, to remind you that in Jesus's death on the cross "the wisdom of God" (1 Cor. 1:24) is on full display. Also ask for help to stand strong when the world mocks these truths as false and foolish.

> Memory Verse
> If any of you lacks wisdom, let him ask God, who gives generously to all without reproach, and it will be given him. (James 1:5)

• • •

"My Song Is Love Unknown"
Samuel Crossman • 1664[19]

My song is love unknown,
My Savior's love to me;
Love to the loveless shown,
That they might lovely be.
O who am I, that for my sake
My Lord should take, frail flesh and die?

Sometimes they strew His way,
And His sweet praises sing;

Resounding all the day
Hosannas to their King:
Then "Crucify!" is all their breath,
And for His death they thirst and cry.

Why, what hath my Lord done?
To cause this rage and spite?
He made the lame to run,
He gave the blind their sight,
Sweet injuries! Yet all his deeds
their hatred feeds; they 'gainst him rise.

Here might I stay and sing,
Of Him my soul adores;
Never was love, dear King!
Never was grief like yours.
This is my Friend, in Whose sweet praise
I all my days could gladly spend.

Wisdom

Part 5 of 5

Adoration
Pray the prayer below. Then pause to praise God for who he is and what he has done.

O Divine Redeemer, great was your goodness in undertaking my redemption, in consenting to be made sin for me, in conquering all my foes. Great was your strength in enduring the extremities of divine wrath, in taking away the load of my iniquities. Great was your love in manifesting yourself alive, in showing your sacred wounds, that every fear might vanish and every doubt be removed. Great was your mercy in ascending to heaven, in being crowned and enthroned there to intercede for me, there to help me in temptation, there to open the eternal book, there to receive me finally to yourself. Great was your wisdom in devising this means of salvation. Bathe my soul in rich consolations of your resurrection life. Great was your grace in commanding me to come hand in hand with you to the Father, to be knit to him eternally, to discover in him my rest, to find in him my peace, to behold his glory, to honor him who is alone worthy; in giving me the Spirit as teacher, guide, power, that I may live repenting of sin, conquer Satan, find victory in life. Amen.
Valley of Vision[20]

Confession
Pray the prayer below. Then take time to ask God through Jesus to forgive specific sins.

Most holy and merciful Father, I acknowledge and confess in your presence my sinful nature, which is quick to do evil and slow to do good, and all my shortcomings and offenses against you. You alone know how often I have sinned in wandering from your ways, in wasting your gifts, in forgetting your love. O Lord, have mercy on me. I admit that I am ashamed and sorry for all things in which I have displeased you. Teach me to know my errors, cleanse me from my secret faults, and forgive my sins for the sake of your dear Son, my Savior. And, most holy and loving Father, send your Holy Spirit into my heart, that I may live in your light and walk in your ways as I seek to follow your Son, the Lord Jesus Christ. Amen.   *Henry Van Dyke*

Thanksgiving
Thank God for the truth that "If we confess our sins, he is faithful and just to forgive us our sins and to cleanse us from all unrighteousness" (1 John 1:9), then pray the prayer below. Finally, take time to thank God for specific blessings in your life. Also feel free to offer Psalm 118:1 ("Oh give thanks to the Lord, for he is good; for his steadfast love endures forever!") as a repeated refrain as you list off (and lift up!) to God people, events, gifts, and circumstances for which you are thankful.

I will praise the name of God with a song;
    I will magnify him with thanksgiving.

I give thanks to you, O Lord my God, with my whole heart,
    and I will glorify your name forever.   *Psalm 69:30; 86:12*[21]

Supplication
After you pray the prayer below, feel free to add your own specific requests.

Lord Jesus, I know what you have clearly taught. When you, the Son of Man, come in your glory with all the angels, you will sit on your glorious throne, and before you all people from all the nations will stand in judgment. Then, my holy and merciful Lord, you will separate believers from unbelievers like a shepherd separates the sheep from the goats. Those who have demonstrated their allegiance to you and your kingdom through care and compassion for the least—such as feeding the hungry, quenching the craving of the thirsty, clothing the naked, visiting the sick and imprisoned, and welcoming the stranger—will be welcomed with the words "Come, you who are blessed by my Father, inherit the kingdom prepared for you from the foundation of the world." Jesus, I know your warnings (of "eternal punishment") and your promises (of "eternal life"). I also know that to love the least in your kingdom is directly to love you. Forgive me for my lack of love for *you*. Forgive me for caring more about myself and my needs than about those in most need. Grant me to walk in a manner worthy of the calling of your gospel.   *Based on Matthew 25:31–46*

Prayer of Illumination

O God, as you instruct your people by your Holy Scriptures, I urge you by your grace to enlighten my mind and cleanse my heart, that, reading, hearing, and meditating upon them, I may rightly understand and heartily embrace the things you have revealed in them. Give efficacy to the reading of the gospel in your word, that through the operation of the Holy Spirit this holy seed may be received into my heart as into good ground; and that I may not only hear your word but keep it living in conformity with your precepts, so that I may finally attain everlasting salvation through Jesus Christ our Lord. Amen.   *Waldensian Liturgy*

· · ·

Scripture Reading

Who is wise and understanding among you? By his good conduct let him show his works in the meekness of wisdom. But if you have bitter jealousy and selfish ambition in your hearts, do not boast and be false to the truth. This is not the wisdom that comes down from above, but is earthly, unspiritual, demonic. For where jealousy and selfish ambition exist, there will be disorder and every vile practice. But the wisdom from above is first pure, then peaceable, gentle, open to reason, full of mercy and good fruits, impartial and sincere. And a harvest of righteousness is sown in peace by those who make peace. *James 3:13–18*

Concise Commentary

In James 1:5–6 James writes, "If any of you lacks wisdom, let him ask God, who gives generously to all without reproach, and it will be given him. But let him ask in faith, with no doubting, for the one who doubts is like a wave of the sea that is driven and tossed by the wind." We should ask in faith for wisdom. But what does such wisdom resemble? How does it manifest itself in our lives? First and foremost it involves fearing God, which, according to the Wisdom Literature of the Bible, includes a continual, humble, and faithful submission to Yahweh that compels us to hate evil and turn away from it, enables us to follow his commands, and brings with it rewards that are better than all earthly treasures—including the rewards of a love for and a knowledge of God. Beyond the fear of the Lord, but always based upon it, is the life of wisdom James describes. In James 3:13–18 he answers the question "Who is wise and understanding among you?" by focusing on "good conduct," notably godly character traits such as meekness, gentleness, reasonableness, peaceability, purity, impartiality, and sincerity. The person who walks in these ways walks in the "wisdom that comes down from above" (3:15). James also describes the opposite of godly wisdom, labeling acts such as "bitter jealousy and selfish ambition," boasting,

and falsehood as "earthly, unspiritual, [even!] demonic" (3:15).
And he reminds us that, if we sow such evil, we will reap "disorder" (3:16); but, if we sow godly wisdom, we can expect a "harvest of righteousness" (3:18). We should choose wisely; we should choose God's wisdom!

Prayer Prompt
Take time to ask God, through his Spirit, to fill you with his wisdom, "wisdom from above," wisdom that is "first pure, then peaceable, gentle, open to reason, full of mercy and good fruits, impartial and sincere" (James 3:17).

> Memory Verse
> If any of you lacks wisdom, let him ask God, who gives generously
> to all without reproach, and it will be given him.   James 1:5

• • •

"I Need Thee Every Hour"
Annie S. Hawks • 1872 | Refrain added by Robert Lowry • 1872

I need Thee ev'ry hour,
Most gracious Lord;
No tender voice like Thine
Can peace afford.

REFRAIN
I need Thee, oh, I need Thee;
Ev'ry hour I need Thee;
Oh, bless me now, my Savior,
I come to Thee.

I need Thee ev'ry hour,
Stay Thou nearby;
Temptations lose their pow'r
When Thou art nigh.

REFRAIN

I need Thee ev'ry hour,
In joy or pain;
Come quickly and abide,
Or life is vain.

REFRAIN

I need Thee ev'ry hour,
Teach me Thy will;
And Thy rich promises
In me fulfill.

REFRAIN

Holiness

Part 1 of 5

Through these biblical and ancient Christian prayers offer your adoration and gratitude to God, confess your sins, and ask for help to read his word and live the Christian life. If it helps, pray aloud and with physical gestures, such as raising your hands (1 Tim. 2:8) when you praise God's holy name or kneeling (Dan. 6:10) or lying prostrate (Luke 5:8) when you confess your sins. Using different postures to pray can engage your body and mind in new ways! "Stand up and bless the LORD your God from everlasting to everlasting" (Neh. 9:5).

Gloria Patri
Pray the Gloria Patri. Then, take time to praise and thank God for specific blessings in your life.

Glory be to the Father, and to the Son, and to the Holy Ghost,
As it was in the beginning, is now, and ever shall be,
    world without end.
Amen.

Agnus Dei
Pray the Agnus Dei. Then take time to ask God through Jesus to forgive specific sins. Also offer prayers of lament. Pray that God would deal with sufferings and injustices both now and when Christ returns. Cry out, "O Sovereign

Lord, holy and true, how long before you will judge and avenge our blood on those who dwell on the earth?" (Rev. 6:10), or *"Out of the depths I cry to you, O Lord! O Lord, hear my voice! Let your ears be attentive to the voice of my pleas for mercy!"* (Ps. 130:1–2).

Lamb of God, who takes away the sins of the world,
    have mercy on us.
Lamb of God, who takes away the sins of the world,
    have mercy on us.
Lamb of God, who takes away the sins of the world,
    grant us peace. Amen.

The Lord's Prayer
Pray each line slowly. As you think about each petition, add your own specific requests.

Our Father in heaven,
hallowed be your name.
Your kingdom come,
your will be done,
    on earth as it is in heaven.
Give us this day our daily bread,
and forgive us our debts,
    as we also have forgiven our debtors.
And lead us not into temptation,
    but deliver us from evil.   *Matthew 6:9–13*

Prayer of Illumination
Lord God Almighty, you alone are holy, holy, holy! As I come now to your holy word, I ask that you would open my eyes to see, my ears to hear, my heart to feel, and my will to obey your will. Amen.

• • •

Scripture Reading

In the year that King Uzziah died I saw the Lord sitting upon a throne, high and lifted up; and the train of his robe filled the temple. Above him stood the seraphim. Each had six wings: with two he covered his face, and with two he covered his feet, and with two he flew. And one called to another and said: "Holy, holy, holy is the LORD of hosts; the whole earth is full of his glory!" And the foundations of the thresholds shook at the voice of him who called, and the house was filled with smoke. And I said: "Woe is me! For I am lost; for I am a man of unclean lips, and I dwell in the midst of a people of unclean lips; for my eyes have seen the King, the LORD of hosts!" Then one of the seraphim flew to me, having in his hand a burning coal that he had taken with tongs from the altar. And he touched my mouth and said: "Behold, this has touched your lips; your guilt is taken away, and your sin atoned for."

Isaiah 6:1–7

Concise Commentary

What is the most amazing thing you have ever seen? A solar eclipse? The Grand Canyon? The stunning beaches of Bora Bora? Take those three amazing sights and multiply them by infinity, and you will get an inch closer to the awesomeness of what Isaiah saw. He saw God! Actually, he saw a vision of God—a dreamlike picture of what God is like. He saw the Lord sitting on an enormous throne lifted high in the air. God was wearing a kingly robe so long that just its hem filled the huge temple. Above God were six-winged angels called seraphim. With two of their wings they flew; with the other four they covered their faces and feet. They covered themselves from head to toe because God was too holy to see. As they flew above him, they called out to one another, "Holy, holy, holy is the LORD of hosts; the whole earth is full of his glory!" (Isa. 6:3). When Isaiah saw this holy King, he cried out, "Woe is me! For I am lost; for I am a man of unclean lips, and I dwell in the midst of a people of unclean lips; for my eyes have seen the King, the LORD of hosts!" (6:5). He recognized that God alone is perfectly holy. He also realized he was not so holy, which terrified him. His unclean lips were just one part of his unclean self. He needed salvation, and he needed it soon! Immediately a seraph swooped down, grabbed a burning coal from the altar, touched Isaiah's mouth, and said, "Your guilt is taken away and your sin completely covered" (see 6:7). This strange picture shows a wonderful truth: only God has the power to take away guilt and sin and make sinners holy. Our gracious and holy God did this for Isaiah, and he has done it for us in Jesus Christ. As Isaiah goes on to predict, "Immanuel" (7:14), which means "God with us," would deliver us through his sufferings (read Isaiah 53!) and sit on David's throne and rule over a never-ending kingdom of peace (9:7). Let us thank our holy God for such a holy Savior.

Prayer Prompt
Take time to thank God for the forgiveness of sins through the sacrifice of Jesus Christ. Also, as Isaiah responded to the Lord's question, "Whom shall I send, and who will go for us?" ask the Spirit to empower you both to say, "Here I am! Send me" (Isa. 6:8), and to take the message of "God with us" to the world.

> Memory Verse
> As obedient children, do not be conformed to the passions of your former ignorance, but as he who called you is holy, you also be holy in all your conduct, since it is written, "You shall be holy, for I am holy." 1 Peter 1:14–16

• • •

"God Himself Is with Us"

Gerhardt Tersteegen · 1729 | *trans. John Miller, Frederick W. Foster* · 1789

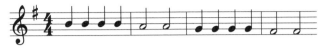

God Himself is with us;
Let us all adore Him,
And with awe appear before Him.
God is here within us;
Soul, in silence fear Him,
Humbly, fervently draw near Him.
Now His own who have known
God, in worship lowly,
Yield their spirits wholly.

Come, abide within me;
Let my soul, like Mary,
Be Thine earthly sanctuary.
Come, indwelling Spirit,
With transfigured splendor;
Love and honor will I render.
Where I go here below,
Let me bow before Thee,
Know Thee and adore Thee.

Gladly we surrender
Earth's deceitful treasures,
Pride of life and sinful pleasures:
Gladly, Lord, we offer
Thine to be forever,
Soul and life and each endeavor.
Thou alone shall be known
Lord of all our being,
Life's true way decreeing.

Holiness
Part 2 of 5

Adoration
Pray the prayer below. Then pause to praise God for who he is and what he has done.

Ascribe to the LORD the glory due his name;
　　bring an offering and come before him!
Worship the LORD in the splendor of holiness;
　　tremble before him, all the earth;
　　yes, the world is established; it shall never be moved.
Let the heavens be glad, and let the earth rejoice,
　　and let them say among the nations, "The LORD reigns!"

Yours, O LORD, is the greatness and the power and the glory and the victory and the majesty, for all that is in the heavens and in the earth is yours. Yours is the kingdom, O LORD, and you are exalted as head above all. Both riches and honor come from you, and you rule over all. In your hand are power and might, and in your hand it is to make great and to give strength to all. And now [I] thank you, [my] God, and praise your glorious name. 1 Chronicles 16:29–31; 29:11–13

Confession
Pray the prayer below. Then take time to ask God through Jesus to forgive specific sins.

I bow before you now, my God, asking you to forgive me for all the ways I have sinned against you. Thank you for such forgiveness. For who is a God like you, pardoning iniquity and passing over transgression for the remnant of his inheritance? You, my gracious God, do not retain your anger forever, because you delight in steadfast love. You will again have compassion on me; you will tread my iniquities underfoot and cast all my sins into the depths of the sea. Thank you. Praise you! You have shown and will continue to show faithfulness to Jacob and steadfast love to Abraham, as you have sworn to our fathers from the days of old. Amen.   *Based on Micah 7:18–20*

Thanksgiving

Thank God for the truth that "If we confess our sins, he is faithful and just to forgive us our sins and to cleanse us from all unrighteousness" (1 John 1:9), then pray the prayer below. Finally, take time to thank God for specific blessings in your life. Also feel free to offer Psalm 118:1 ("Oh give thanks to the LORD, *for he is good; for his steadfast love endures forever!") as a repeated refrain as you list off (and lift up!) to God people, events, gifts, and circumstances for which you are thankful.*

Lord, Most High, you are my God, and I will give thanks to you; you are my God, and I will extol you; you are my God, and I will sing praise to your name. I give thanks with my whole heart, and I will glorify your name forever, for you are good and righteous, and your steadfast love is great above the heavens; your faithfulness reaches to the clouds. Amen.   *Based on Psalms 7:17; 54:6; 108:4; 118:28*

Supplication

After you pray the prayer below, feel free to add your own specific requests.

Give me a deeper trust, that I may lose myself to find myself in you, the ground of my rest, the spring of my being. Give me a deeper knowledge of yourself as Savior, Master, Lord, and King. Give me deeper power in private prayers, more sweetness in your word, more steadfast grip on its truth. Give me deeper holiness in speech, thought, and action, and let me not seek godly virtues apart from you. Amen.   *Valley of Vision*[22]

Prayer of Illumination
Blessed Father, I could never praise you or thank you enough for the glorious reality of your word—the economy of grace that it reveals, the hope of glory that it unfolds, the promises new and strong and unbreakable and rewarding every day. Thank you! As I now open your word, open my eyes to see you better, and soften my heart to love you more and more. Amen.   J. I. Packer[23]

+ + +

Scripture Reading
After this I looked, and behold, a door standing open in heaven! And the first voice, which I had heard speaking to me like a trumpet, said, "Come up here, and I will show you what must take place after this." At once I was in the Spirit, and behold, a throne stood in heaven, with one seated on the throne. And he who sat there had the appearance of jasper and carnelian, and around the throne was a rainbow that had the appearance of an emerald. Around the throne were twenty-four thrones, and seated on the thrones were twenty-four elders, clothed in white garments, with golden crowns on their heads. From the throne came flashes of lightning, and rumblings and peals of thunder, and before the throne were burning seven torches of fire, which are the seven spirits of God, and before the throne there was as it were a sea of glass, like crystal. And around the throne, on each side of the throne, are four living creatures, full of eyes in front and behind: the first living creature like a lion, the second living creature like an ox, the third living creature with the face of a man, and the fourth living

creature like an eagle in flight. And the four living creatures, each of them with six wings, are full of eyes all around and within, and day and night they never cease to say, "Holy, holy, holy, is the Lord God Almighty, who was and is and is to come!" And whenever the living creatures give glory and honor and thanks to him who is seated on the throne, who lives forever and ever, the twenty-four elders fall down before him who is seated on the throne and worship him who lives forever and ever. They cast their crowns before the throne, saying, "Worthy are you, our Lord and God, to receive glory and honor and power, for you created all things, and by your will they existed and were created."   *Revelation 4:1–11*

Concise Commentary

Revelation 4 records John's dreamlike vision. He sees an opened door to heaven. He walks through, and he hears again the voice that sounds like a trumpet. It is Jesus's voice! "Come up here," Jesus says, "and I will show you what must take place" (Rev. 4:1). The next thing you know, God the Spirit has taken John to the throne room of God the Father. John sees a vision of "one seated on the throne" (4:2), who looks like jasper and carnelian and emerald—beautiful, colorful, and expensive stones. Of course, God is not literally sitting on some throne that looks like three stones, as God does not have a body and thus does not need something to sit on. The throne symbolizes God's power and control; the stones his beauty and mercy. "From the throne came flashes of lightning" and "peals of thunder," and "before the throne" everything was still, as though it were a "sea of glass" (4:5–6). Power and peace. John sees incredible creatures, too. Surrounding the throne are four living creatures who have six wings and eyes on every part of their bodies, and all they do day and night is sing, "Holy, holy, holy, is the Lord God Almighty" (4:8). Circling the throne are twenty-four elders seated on twenty-four thrones, wearing white garments and gold crowns. These figures cast their crowns before their Creator and say, "Worthy are you, our Lord and God, to receive glory and honor and power, for you created all things, and by your will they existed and were created" (4:11).

Prayer Prompt

Take time to ask the Father to help you see something of his holiness so that you might join those "heavenly beings" (angels and those who cast their crowns before him and worship him), adding to their words those of the psalmist, "Ascribe to the LORD the glory due his name," and "worship the LORD in the splendor of holiness" (Ps. 29:2).

Memory Verse

As obedient children, do not be conformed to the passions of your former ignorance, but as he who called you is holy, you also be holy in all your conduct, since it is written, "You shall be holy, for I am holy." 1 Peter 1:14–16

◆ ◆ ◆

"Holy, Holy, Holy"
Reginald Heber · 1826

Holy, holy, holy! Lord God Almighty!
Early in the morning our song shall rise to Thee;
Holy, holy, holy! merciful and mighty!
God in three Persons, bless-ed Trinity!

Holy, holy, holy! all the saints adore Thee,
casting down their golden crowns around the glassy sea;
cherubim and seraphim, falling down before Thee,
which wert and art and evermore shalt be.

Holy, holy, holy! though the darkness hide Thee,
though the eye of sinful man Thy glory may not see;
only Thou art holy, there is none beside Thee,
perfect in pow'r, in love, and purity.

Holy, holy, holy! Lord God Almighty!
All Thy works shall praise Thy name, in earth and sky and sea;
Holy, holy, holy! merciful and mighty!
God in three Persons, blessed Trinity!

Holiness

Part 3 of 5

Adoration

Pray the prayer below. Then pause to praise God for who he is and what he has done.

You alone rest highest among the highest, holy among the holy. You lay low the insolence of the haughty, set the low on high, and bring down the exalted. You make rich and make poor, kill and make to live. You are the only benefactor of spirits and the God of all flesh. Amen.   *Clement of Rome*

Confession

Pray the prayer below. Then take time to ask God through Jesus to forgive specific sins.

O King eternal, immortal, invisible, and only wise God, before whom angels bow and seraphs veil their faces, crying holy, holy, holy is the Lord God Almighty: true and righteous are your ways, King of saints. Help me, your poor and needy creature, humbly to prostrate myself before you and to implore that mercy that my sins have justly forfeited. O God, I know that I am not worthy of a place at your footstool; but to whom shall I go but unto you? You alone have the words of eternal life. Send me not away without a blessing, I beg you, but enable me to wrestle like

Jacob and to prevail like Israel. Be graciously pleased, O God, to pardon all that you have seen amiss in me this day, and enable me to live more to your honor and glory for the time to come. Amen.   *Maria W. Stewart*

Thanksgiving
Thank God for the truth that "If we confess our sins, he is faithful and just to forgive us our sins and to cleanse us from all unrighteousness" (1 John 1:9), then pray the prayer below. Finally, take time to thank God for specific blessings in your life. Also feel free to offer Psalm 118:1 ("Oh give thanks to the Lord, *for he is good; for his steadfast love endures forever!") as a repeated refrain as you list off (and lift up!) to God people, events, gifts, and circumstances for which you are thankful.*

Lord Jesus, Great High Priest, you have opened a new and living way by which a fallen creature can approach you with acceptance. Thank you. Give me a heart filled with gratitude as I contemplate the dignity of your person, the perfections of your sacrifice, and the effectiveness of your intercession. Amen.   *Valley of Vision*[24]

Supplication
After you pray the prayer below, feel free to add your own specific requests.

O Lord, receive me in repentance; O Lord, leave me not; O Lord, save me from temptation; O Lord, grant me pure thoughts; O Lord, grant me tears of repentance, remembrance of death, and the sense of peace; O Lord, grant me mindfulness to confess my sins; O Lord, grant me humility, charity, and obedience; O Lord, grant me generosity and gentleness; O Lord, implant in me the root of all blessings: the fear of you in my heart; O Lord, grant that I may love you with all my heart and soul, and that I may obey your will; O Lord, shield me from evil persons and devils and passions and all other lawless matters; O Lord, who knows your creation and that which you have willed for it, may

your will also be fulfilled in me, a sinner, for you are blessed forevermore. Amen.   *John Chrysostom*

Prayer of Illumination
Send your Holy Spirit into my mind and give me grace to learn
the divine Scriptures from the Holy Spirit and to interpret,
cleanly and worthily, that when I converse with others about
your word or teach it, they may be helped, through your only
begotten Son Jesus Christ in the Holy Spirit, through whom to
you be the glory and the strength both now and to all the ages
of the ages. Amen.   *Serapion Scholasticus*

• • •

Scripture Reading
And Hannah prayed and said,

"My heart exults in the LORD;
    my horn is exalted in the LORD.
My mouth derides my enemies,
    because I rejoice in your salvation.
There is none holy like the LORD:
    for there is none besides you;
    there is no rock like our God.
Talk no more so very proudly,
    let not arrogance come from your mouth;
    for the LORD is a God of knowledge,
    and by him actions are weighed.
The bows of the mighty are broken,
    but the feeble bind on strength.
Those who were full have hired themselves out for bread,
    but those who were hungry have ceased to hunger.
The barren has borne seven,
    but she who has many children is forlorn.

The LORD kills and brings to life;
    he brings down to Sheol and raises up.
The LORD makes poor and makes rich;
    he brings low and he exalts.
He raises up the poor from the dust;
    he lifts the needy from the ash heap
to make them sit with princes
    and inherit a seat of honor.
For the pillars of the earth are the LORD's,
    and on them he has set the world.
He will guard the feet of his faithful ones,
    but the wicked shall be cut off in darkness,
    for not by might shall a man prevail.
The adversaries of the LORD shall be broken to pieces;
    against them he will thunder in heaven.
The LORD will judge the ends of the earth;
    he will give strength to his king
    and exalt the horn of his anointed." *1 Samuel 2:1–10*

Concise Commentary

The first chapter of 1 Samuel begins with the plight, promise, and praise of Hannah. Her *plight* is her barrenness; her *promise* is that, if God will give her a son, she will "give him to the LORD all the days of his life" (1:11); and her *praise* is when she worships the Lord for remembering her when Samuel is born (1:19–20). Chapter 2 starts with her *prayer*, also called Hannah's hymn. It is a song that sings of the way God has worked in the past (2:1–2), works in the present (2:3–8), and will work in the future (2:9–10). But it is more than a song that celebrates the mighty acts of God; it also celebrates the attributes of "the LORD" (Yahweh, 46x in 1 Sam. 1–2): his holiness, uniqueness, strength, knowledge, sovereignty, and justice. Hannah begins with God's holiness ("There is none holy like the LORD," 2:2) and ends with God's justice ("The LORD will judge the ends of the earth," 2:10a). Here, as throughout the

Bible, a holy God saves his unholy people from the coming judgment by means of the Christ ("He will give strength to his king and exalt the horn of his anointed," v. 10b).

What starts as a song about Hannah's personal salvation (her deliverance from barrenness) ends with a song the celebrates the culmination of the world's salvation through Israel's promised king. This theme fits within the scroll of 1–2 Samuel (originally one book), where near the beginning we have the Song of Hannah (1 Sam. 2) and near the end the Song of David (2 Sam. 22), two songs that sing of the theme of salvation through the anointed king. The theme also fits within the context of the books of Judges and Ruth. Judges can be summarized as *there was no king* ("In those days there was no king in Israel. Everyone did what was right in his own eyes," Judg. 21:25), Ruth as *here comes the king* ("Obed fathered Jesse, and Jesse fathered David," Ruth 4:22), and 1–2 Samuel as *here is the king*, since these books tell us the story of the rise of King David. Of course, we know about the bigger story and the grander salvation in Jesus, the "righteous Branch" (Jer. 23:5), "the root and the descendant of David" (Rev. 22:16), the "Christ, the son of David" (Matt. 1:1), whose reign will be one of eternal peace ("of peace there will be no end"), justice, and righteousness ("on the throne of David and over his kingdom, to establish it and to uphold it with justice and with righteousness from this time forth and forevermore," Isa. 9:7).[25]

Prayer Prompt
Take time to praise the Lord that he has provided "a Savior, Jesus, as he promised" (Acts 13:23) and given to him "the throne of his father David," a kingdom by which "he will reign over the house of Jacob forever" (Luke 1:33). Join your voice with the crowd ("Hosanna to the Son of David! . . . Hosanna in the highest!," Matt. 21:9), with Zechariah ("Blessed be the Lord God of Israel, for he has visited and redeemed his people and has raised up a

horn of salvation for us in the house of his servant David," Luke 1:68–69), and with Mary ("My soul magnifies the Lord," 1:46).

> Memory Verse
> As obedient children, do not be conformed to the passions of your former ignorance, but as he who called you is holy, you also be holy in all your conduct, since it is written, "You shall be holy, for I am holy." 1 Peter 1:14–16

• • •

"Let All Mortal Flesh Keep Silence"
Liturgy of St. James • 5th. cent. | Adapted by Gerard Moultrie • 1864

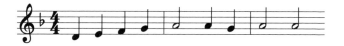

Let all mortal flesh keep silence,
and with fear and trembling stand;
ponder nothing earthly minded,
for, with blessing in His hand,
Christ our God to earth descendeth,
our full homage to demand.

King of kings, yet born of Mary,
as of old on earth He stood,
Lord of lords, in human vesture,
in the body and the blood.
He will give to all the faithful
His own self for heav'nly food.

Rank on rank the host of heaven
spreads its vanguard on the way,
as the Light of light descendeth

from the realms of endless day,
that the pow'rs of hell may vanish
as the darkness clears away.

At His feet the six-winged seraph,
cherubim with sleepless eye,
veil their faces to the Presence,
as with ceaseless voice they cry,
"Alleluia, alleluia,
alleluia, Lord Most High!"

Holiness

Part 4 of 5

Adoration
Pray the prayer below. Then pause to praise God for who he is and what he has done.

Praise the LORD!
Praise God in his sanctuary;
    praise him in his mighty heavens!
Praise him for his mighty deeds;
    praise him according to his excellent greatness!
Praise him with trumpet sound;
    praise him with lute and harp!
Praise him with tambourine and dance;
    praise him with strings and pipe!
Praise him with sounding cymbals;
    praise him with loud clashing cymbals!
Let everything that has breath praise the LORD!
Praise the LORD!   *Psalm 150:1–6*

Confession
Pray the prayer below. Then take time to ask God through Jesus to forgive specific sins.

Loving heavenly Father, you have dealt kindly and patiently with me, and I should worship you alone, with joy and gratitude, every moment of every day. Your word should delight me, and your law should motivate me to obedience, all day, every day. Yet, Lord, I am a great sinner, who wanders and runs from you often. I regularly exchange your truth for lies because I do not want to worship and obey you. Rather, I want to be my own ruler, my own god! Many times each day I turn from you toward the idols that enchant me, bowing before them and hoping that they will make me happy or bring me some peace. I will admit that too often I treasure your gifts (my gods of worship) instead of treasuring you. O Father—my loving heavenly Father!—have mercy on me, for I am weak and always in need of your new morning and afternoon and evening mercies. Amen. Barbara R. Duguid[26]

Thanksgiving
Thank God for the truth that "If we confess our sins, he is faithful and just to forgive us our sins and to cleanse us from all unrighteousness" (1 John 1:9), then pray the prayer below. Finally, take time to thank God for specific blessings in your life. Also feel free to offer Psalm 118:1 ("Oh give thanks to the Lord, for he is good; for his steadfast love endures forever!") as a repeated refrain as you list off (and lift up!) to God people, events, gifts, and circumstances for which you are thankful.

Father in heaven, I thank you for the excellencies of Jesus, your Son and my Savior. I thank you for his immeasurable highness and inestimable condescension; his infinite justice and infinite grace; his utmost glory and lowest humility; his greatest majesty and transcendent meekness; his deepest reverence toward you and yet equality with you; his vast worthiness of good and the utmost patience under sufferings of evil; his exceeding spirit of obedience, with supreme dominion over heaven and earth; his absolute sovereignty and perfect resignation; and his self-sufficiency and entire trust and reliance on you. To him, with you and the Spirit, be all glory forever and ever. Amen.   *Jonathan Edwards*

Supplication

After you pray the prayer below, feel free to add your own specific requests.

O Lord, come quickly and reign on your throne, for now these things often rise up within me and try to take possession of your throne; pride, covetousness, uncleanness, and sloth want to be my kings, and then evil-speaking, anger, hatred, and the whole train of vices join with me in warring against myself, and they try to reign over me. I resist them; I cry out against them and say, "I have no other king than Christ." O King of peace, come and reign in me, for I will have no king but you! Amen.   *Bernard of Clairvaux*

Prayer of Illumination

On the first day of creation, Lord, you caused light to shine out of the darkness. On this new day, Lord, open the heavens and shine down your light on my heart, so I might see, know, love, and obey your word. Amen.

◆ ◆ ◆

Scripture Reading

As obedient children, do not be conformed to the passions of your former ignorance, but as he who called you is holy, you also be holy in all your conduct, since it is written, "You shall be holy, for I am holy." And if you call on him as Father who judges impartially according to each one's deeds, conduct yourselves with fear throughout the time of your exile, knowing that you were ransomed from the futile ways inherited from your forefathers, not with perishable things such as silver or gold, but with the precious blood of Christ, like that of a lamb without blemish or spot. He was foreknown before the foundation of the world but was made manifest in the last times for the sake of you who through him are believers in God, who raised him from the dead and gave him glory, so that your faith and hope are in God.

Having purified your souls by your obedience to the truth for a sincere brotherly love, love one another earnestly from a pure heart, since you have been born again, not of perishable seed but of imperishable, through the living and abiding word of God; for

"All flesh is like grass
        and all its glory like the flower of grass.
The grass withers,
        and the flower falls,
but the word of the Lord remains forever."

And this word is the good news that was preached to you.

1 Peter 1:14–25

Concise Commentary

First Peter 1 begins and ends with the gospel. The final verse speaks of the "good news [*euangelisthen*] that was preached to you" (1:25), and the first section (1:1–12) offers the details of that good news, ending with a similar line: "The things that have now been announced to you through those who preached the good news [*euangelisamenōn*] to you" (1:12). That good news is that we have been born again and have a living hope of heaven, where we will experience "an inheritance that is imperishable, undefiled, and unfading"; due to that future hope, our present faith sustains us through "various trials" (1:6). It also equips us to live holy lives. Verse 13 begins the important transition from the objectivity of the gospel ("Therefore, preparing your minds for action, and being sober-minded, set your hope fully on the grace that will be brought to you at the revelation of Jesus Christ") to the call to Christian holiness ("As obedient children, do not be conformed to the passions of your former ignorance, but as he who called you is holy, you also be holy in all your conduct," 1:14–15). That command is grounded in what "the Lord spoke to Moses" in Leviticus 19:1–2: "You shall be holy, for I the LORD your

God am holy," or, as Peter summarizes, "You shall be holy, for I am holy" (1 Pet. 1:16). In the context of Leviticus holiness means observing all God's commandments over every sphere of life, grounded in God's mercy (in the Israelites' case, shown in their deliverance from the bondage of slavery in Egypt) and expressed in love of others (Lev. 19:18). Similarly, Peter speaks of Christians' being "ransomed . . . with the precious blood of Christ, like that of a lamb without blemish or spot" (1 Pet. 1:18–19) and for the purpose of expressing a holy life through a loving life ("Love one another earnestly from a pure heart," 1:21).

Prayer Prompt
Take time to ask God, through his Spirit, to help you hold firm to the truth of the living and abiding word of God and to help you to walk in a manner worthy of the gospel—to walk in holiness and love.

Memory Verse
As obedient children, do not be conformed to the passions of your former ignorance, but as he who called you is holy, you also be holy in all your conduct, since it is written, "You shall be holy, for I am holy." 1 Peter 1:14–16

• • •

"Holy God, We Praise Your Name"
Based on Te Deum • *4th cent.* | *Attributed to Ignace Franz* • *c. 1774*
trans. Clarence A. Walworth • *1853*

Holy God, we praise Your name;
Lord of all, we bow before You.

Saints on earth Your scepter claim;
all in heav'n above adore You.
Infinite, Your vast domain;
everlasting is Your reign.

Hark, the glad celestial hymn
angel choirs above are raising;
cherubim and seraphim,
in unceasing chorus praising,
fill the heav'ns with sweet accord:
"Holy, holy, holy Lord!"

Lo, the apostolic train
joins Your sacred name to hallow;
prophets swell the glad refrain,
and the white-robed martyrs follow;
and from morn to set of sun,
through the church the song goes on.

Holy Father, Holy Son,
Holy Spirit, three we name You,
though in essence only one;
undivided God, we claim You,
and, adoring, bend the knee
while we own the mystery.

Holiness

Part 5 of 5

Adoration

Pray the prayer below. Then pause to praise God for who he is and what he has done.

The LORD reigns; let the peoples tremble!
    He sits enthroned upon the cherubim; let the earth quake!
The LORD is great in Zion;
    he is exalted over all the peoples.
Let them praise your great and awesome name!
    Holy is he!
The King in his might loves justice.
    You have established equity;
you have executed justice
    and righteousness in Jacob.
Exalt the LORD our God;
    worship at his footstool!
    Holy is he!

Exalt the LORD our God,
    and worship at his holy mountain;
    for the LORD our God is holy!   *Psalm 99:1–5, 9*

Confession

Pray the prayer below. Then take time to ask God through Jesus to forgive specific sins.

Lord, for the times I have sinned against you with my impure
      thoughts, words, and actions,
  forgive me, Lord.
Lord, for the times I have been dishonest and duplicitous,
  forgive me, Lord.
Lord, for the times I have oppressed and exploited others,
  forgive me, Lord.
Lord, for the times I have been an idolater—putting other
      people, places, and things above you,
  forgive me, Lord.
Lord, for the times I have been vindictive,
  forgive me, Lord.
Lord, for the times I have been inhospitable,
  forgive me, Lord.   *Based on Job 31:24–40*

Thanksgiving

Thank God for the truth that "If we confess our sins, he is faithful and just to forgive us our sins and to cleanse us from all unrighteousness" (1 John 1:9), then pray the prayer below. Finally, take time to thank God for specific blessings in your life. Also feel free to offer Psalm 118:1 ("Oh give thanks to the Lord, *for he is good; for his steadfast love endures forever!") as a repeated refrain as you list off (and lift up!) to God people, events, gifts, and circumstances for which you are thankful.*

Father in heaven, I thank you for your Son, Jesus. Although he is the light of the world, full of glory and grace, he volunteered to enter our darkness and live in our flesh and blood to destroy the power of sin over us. He lived his life in shining obedience so that he could give his goodness to your people as a free gift. He chose to be slain by the darkness in order

to pay our debt, and I am undone by his sacrifice. Amen.
Barbara R. Duguid[27]

Supplication
After you pray the prayer below, feel free to add your own specific requests.

Spirit of God, you are the Wisdom of heaven, never leading us into folly. Spirit of God, you are a Spirit of Love, delighting always to do good. Spirit of God, you are a Spirit of Concord, ever for the unity of believers, abhorring division. Spirit of God, you are a Spirit of Humility and Self-Denial, making us little in our own eyes, abhorring pride. Spirit of God, you are a Spirit of Meekness, for patience and forbearance, abhorring envy. Spirit of God, you are a Spirit of Zeal for God, resolving us against known sin, abhorring indifference. Spirit of God, you are a Spirit of Mortification, contending against the flesh, abhorring selfish license. Spirit of God, may I never quench your influence in my life, either by willful sin or by neglecting your help. You are the spring to all your spiritual motions; I can do nothing without you. Therefore, I pray for your help. May I not neglect the means you have appointed; let me be constant in prayer, meditation, hearing, reading, expecting your blessing. Like a farmer who plows and sows, expecting the sun and rain to yield a harvest, may I sow according to your appointed means, and may you grant in us a harvest of life and holiness. Amen.   *Richard Baxter*

Prayer of Illumination
I know, O Lord, and tremble to think that three parts of the good seed falls upon bad ground. O let not my heart be like the path, which, through hardness and want of true understanding, receives not the seed before the evil one comes and snatches it away. Nor like the stony ground, which bears with joy for a time but falls away as soon as persecution arises for the gospel's sake. Nor like the thorny ground, which, by the cares

of this world and the deceitfulness of riches, chokes the word, making it altogether unfruitful. But, like the good ground, may I hear your word (with an honest and good heart), understand it, keep it, and bring forth fruit with patience, in the measaure that your wisdom finds fitting for your glory and my everlasting comfort. Amen.   *Lewis Bayly*

• • •

Scripture Reading

This is the message we have heard from him and proclaim to you, that God is light, and in him is no darkness at all. If we say we have fellowship with him while we walk in darkness, we lie and do not practice the truth. But if we walk in the light, as he is in the light, we have fellowship with one another, and the blood of Jesus his Son cleanses us from all sin. If we say we have no sin, we deceive ourselves, and the truth is not in us. If we confess our sins, he is faithful and just to forgive us our sins and to cleanse us from all unrighteousness. If we say we have not sinned, we make him a liar, and his word is not in us.   1 John 1:5–10

Concise Commentary

In the fourth century a scribe copying what we now call "Revelation" wrote atop the first page, "A Revelation of John." He also wrote in the margin the Greek words *tou theologou* ("the theologian"). After a prologue (1 John 1:1–4) the body of the theologian's first letter begins with a proclamation (or the heralding of a royal decree!) that describes God: "This is the message we [the apostles] have heard from him [Jesus] and proclaim to you, that God is light, and in him is no darkness at all" (1:5). God "is light" in the sense that he is perfectly pure both morally (no evil/all good) and intellectually (no error/all truth). As verse 9 clarifies, "light" equals "faithful" (God does what he says he will do) and "just" (he does so in absolute righteousness). That perfect purity is emphasized with the double negative in Greek and the synthetic parallelism below (where the first idea in the first line is expanded upon or further explained in the second line):

God	is	light,
in him	is	no darkness at all [none]

In light of that Light, and as "children of the light" (1 Thess. 5:5), we are called to "walk in the light" (1 John 1:7). Later John will explain how this entails a life of lawfulness (2:1–6) and love (2:7–11). Here, however, he teaches that our first step on the right (and "light"!) path is to recognize the darkness within. A proper assessment of self and sin—where we say neither "we have no sin" nor "we have not sinned" but rather "we have sin" and "we still sin"—should lead to a life of consistently contrite confessions whereby the Father's forgiveness is given and our fellowship with God and others, by the blood of Christ and the ministry of the Spirit, is renewed. God's holiness (he is light) shows our unholiness (we are stained with sin) and thus our need of an incarnate and crucified Christ (who is light and love) to wash us in his holy blood.[28]

Prayer Prompt

Take time to ask God to help you see him as pure light, to acknowledge your stain of sin, and to be grateful for the forgiveness offered in Jesus Christ. Ask for the Spirit's help to walk in the light, as the Father, Son, and Spirit are in the light.

Memory Verse

As obedient children, do not be conformed to the passions of your former ignorance, but as he who called you is holy, you also be holy in all your conduct, since it is written, "You shall be holy, for I am holy." 1 Peter 1:14–16

♦ ♦ ♦

"The God of Abraham Praise"
Daniel ben Judah · c. 1400 | paraphrased by Thomas Olivers · 1770

The God of Abraham praise,
who reigns enthroned above;
Ancient of Everlasting Days,
and God of Love;
Jehovah, great I AM!
by earth and heaven confessed;
I bow and bless the sacred name
forever blest.

He by Himself has sworn;
I on His oath depend,
I shall, on eagle wings upborne,
to Heav'n ascend.
I shall behold His face;
I shall His pow'r adore,
And sing the wonders of His grace
forevermore.

The God who reigns on high
the great archangels sing,
and "Holy, holy, holy!" cry
"Almighty King!
Who was, and is, the same,
and evermore shall be:
Jehovah, Lord, the great I AM,
we worship Thee!"

The whole triumphant host
give thanks to God on high;

"Hail, Father, Son, and Holy Ghost,"
they ever cry.
Hail, Abraham's God, and mine!
(I join the heav'nly lays,)
All might and majesty are Thine,
and endless praise.

Perseverance

Part 1 of 5

Through these biblical and ancient Christian prayers offer your adoration and gratitude to God, confess your sins, and ask for help to read his word and live the Christian life. If it helps, pray aloud and with physical gestures, such as raising your hands (1 Tim. 2:8) when you praise God's holy name or kneeling (Dan. 6:10) or lying prostrate (Luke 5:8) when you confess your sins. Using different postures to pray can engage your body and mind in new ways! "Stand up and bless the LORD your God from everlasting to everlasting" (Neh. 9:5).

Gloria Patri
Pray the Gloria Patri. Then, take time to praise and thank God for specific blessings in your life.

Glory be to the Father, and to the Son, and to the Holy Ghost,
As it was in the beginning, is now, and ever shall be,
    world without end.
Amen.

Agnus Dei
Pray the Agnus Dei. Then take time to ask God through Jesus to forgive specific sins. Also offer prayers of lament. Pray that God would deal with sufferings and injustices both now and when Christ returns. Cry out, "O Sovereign

Lord, holy and true, how long before you will judge and avenge our blood on those who dwell on the earth?" (Rev. 6:10), or "Out of the depths I cry to you, O LORD! O Lord, hear my voice! Let your ears be attentive to the voice of my pleas for mercy!" (Ps. 130:1–2).

Lamb of God, who takes away the sins of the world,
    have mercy on us.
Lamb of God, who takes away the sins of the world,
    have mercy on us.
Lamb of God, who takes away the sins of the world,
    grant us peace. Amen.

The Lord's Prayer
Pray each line slowly. As you think about each petition, add your own specific requests.

Our Father in heaven,
hallowed be your name.
Your kingdom come,
your will be done,
    on earth as it is in heaven.
Give us this day our daily bread,
and forgive us our debts,
    as we also have forgiven our debtors.
And lead us not into temptation,
    but deliver us from evil.   Matthew 6:9–13

Prayer of Illumination
With my whole heart I seek you;
    let me not wander from your commandments!
Blessed are you, O LORD;
    teach me your statutes!
Make me understand the way of your precepts,
    and I will meditate on your wondrous works.

My soul melts away for sorrow;
    strengthen me according to your word!
Put false ways far from me
    and graciously teach me your law!
I will run in the way of your commandments
    when you enlarge my heart!
Teach me, O LORD, the way of your statutes;
    and I will keep it to the end.
Give me understanding, that I may keep your law
    and observe it with my whole heart.
Lead me in the path of your commandments,
    for I delight in it.
Incline my heart to your testimonies,
    and not to selfish gain!
Turn my eyes from looking at worthless things;
    and give me life in your ways.   *Psalm* 119:10, 12, 27–29, 32, 33–37

• • •

Scripture Reading

And when they had crucified him, they divided his garments among them by casting lots. Then they sat down and kept watch over him there. And over his head they put the charge against him, which read, "This is Jesus, the King of the Jews." Then two robbers were crucified with him, one on the right and one on the left. And those who passed by derided him, wagging their heads and saying, "You who would destroy the temple and rebuild it in three days, save yourself! If you are the Son of God, come down from the cross." So also the chief priests, with the scribes and elders, mocked him, saying, "He saved others; he cannot save himself. He is the King of Israel; let him come down now from the cross, and we will believe in him. He trusts in God; let God deliver him now, if he desires him. For he said, 'I am the Son of God.'" And the robbers who were crucified with him also reviled him in the same way.

Now from the sixth hour there was darkness over all the land until the ninth hour. And about the ninth hour Jesus cried out with a loud voice, saying, "Eli, Eli, lema sabachthani?" that is, "My God, my God, why have you forsaken me?" And some of the bystanders, hearing it, said, "This man is calling Elijah." And one of them at once ran and took a sponge, filled it with sour wine, and put it on a reed and gave it to him to drink. But the others said, "Wait, let us see whether Elijah will come to save him." And Jesus cried out again with a loud voice and yielded up his spirit.
Matthew 27:35–50

Concise Commentary

Just as Jesus called his disciples to do "the will of [his] Father who is in heaven" (Matt. 7:21), he alone perfectly fulfilled that calling. Through Jesus's words and works and the total constancy of his character, Matthew presents Jesus as the embodiment of perfect faithfulness, as demonstrated in trust in God and fidelity to God's plan. This faithfulness is epitomized in Jesus's two great temptations, when he overcame Satan ("Be gone, Satan!" 4:10) and Peter's satanic suggestion to take the crown without the cross (see 16:23). Indeed, it is illustrated best when his deriders, as Jesus dies on the cross, call out, "He saved others; he cannot save himself. He is the King of Israel; let him come down now from the cross, and we will believe in him. He trusts in God; let God deliver him now, if he desires him. For he said, 'I am the Son of God'" (27:42–43). "Trust" is a good translation of the Greek word *pepoithen*, although adding the adjective "tenacious" sharpens the sense of the word, since this verse ironically highlights Jesus's total commitment to the Father and the Father's will—his fulfillment of his Gethsemane prayer ("My Father, if it be possible, let this cup pass from me; nevertheless, not as I will, but as you will," 26:39). Jesus's faithfulness knows no limits; he is obedient unto death! He is the ultimate "good and faithful servant" who receives God's highest commendation ("well done,"

25:21, 23) and in due course the vindication of his glorious resurrection and eternal reign. The author of Hebrews picks up on this theme when he speaks of Jesus as the one who "for the joy that was set before him endured the cross, despising the shame, and is seated at the right hand of the throne of God," and thus the author invites us to look to Jesus as we "run with endurance the race that is set before us" (Heb. 12:1–2).

Prayer Prompt
Take time to ask God, through his Spirit, to help you to heed the "call for the endurance of the saints" through "faith in Jesus" (Rev. 14:12), our "Faithful and True" King (19:11).

Memory Verse
Since then we have a great high priest who has passed through the heavens, Jesus, the Son of God, let us hold fast our confession.
Hebrews 4:14

• • •

"The Church's One Foundation"
Samuel John Stone · 1866

The church's one foundation
is Jesus Christ, her Lord;
she is His new creation,
by water and the word
From heav'n He came and sought her
to be His holy bride;
with His own blood He bought her,
and for her life He died.

Elect from every nation,
yet one o'er all the earth,
her charter of salvation:
one Lord, one faith, one birth.
One holy name she blesses,
partakes one holy food,
and to one hope she presses,
with every grace endued.

Though with a scornful wonder,
men see her sore oppressed,
by schisms rent asunder,
by heresies distressed,
yet saints their watch are keeping,
their cry goes up, "How long?"
and soon the night of weeping
shall be the morn of song!

'Mid toil and tribulation,
and tumult of her war,
she waits the consummation
of peace forevermore;
till with the vision glorious
her longing eyes are blest,
and the great church victorious
shall be the church at rest.

Yet she on earth hath union
with God the Three in One,
and mystic sweet communion
with those whose rest is won;
O happy ones and holy!
Lord give us grace that we,
like them, the meek and lowly,
on high may dwell with Thee.

Perseverance

Part 2 of 5

Adoration
Pray the prayer below. Then pause to praise God for who he is and what he has done.

I will bless the LORD at all times;
    his praise shall continually be in my mouth.

I sought the LORD, and he answered me
    and delivered me from all my fears.   Psalm 34:1, 4

Confession
Pray the prayer below. Then take time to ask God through Jesus to forgive specific sins.

Heavenly Father, I confess to you that I am often proud and self-dependent and not poor in spirit. I defend my own rights and reputation rather than demonstrating meekness. I hunger and thirst for getting my own way instead of for your righteousness. I forget the mercy that I have received and so show little mercy to others. I have jealous thoughts that lead to strife instead of pursuing your peace. For the sake of your son, Jesus, have mercy on me and forgive me, that by your Spirit I may delight in your will and walk in your ways, to the glory of your name. Amen.[29]

Thanksgiving

Thank God for the truth that "If we confess our sins, he is faithful and just to forgive us our sins and to cleanse us from all unrighteousness" (1 John 1:9), then pray the prayer below. Finally, take time to thank God for specific blessings in your life. Also feel free to offer Psalm 118:1 ("Oh give thanks to the Lord, *for he is good; for his steadfast love endures forever!") as a repeated refrain as you list off (and lift up!) to God people, events, gifts, and circumstances for which you are thankful.*

Eternal Light, you have shone into my heart the truth of the gospel. Thank you. Eternal Goodness, you have delivered me from evil. Thank you. Eternal Power, you have been my support. Thank you. Eternal Wisdom, you have scattered the darkness of my ignorance. Thank you. Eternal Pity, you have had mercy on me, that with all my heart and mind and soul and strength I may seek your face and be brought by your infinite mercy into your holy presence, through Jesus Christ our Lord. Thank you. Amen.   *Alcuin of York*

Supplication

After you pray the prayer below, feel free to add your own specific requests.

God of all grace, you have given me a Savior; produce in me a faith to live by him, to make him all my desire, all my hope, all my glory. May I shelter in him as my refuge, build on him as my foundation, walk in him as my way, follow him as my guide, conform to him as my example, receive his instructions as my prophet, rely on his intercession as my high priest, obey him as my king. May I never be ashamed of him or his words but joyfully bear his reproach, never displease him by unholy or imprudent conduct, never count it a glory if I take it patiently when buffeted for a fault, never make the multitude my model, never delay when your word invites me to advance. May your dear Son preserve me from this present evil world, so that its smiles never allure, nor its frowns terrify, nor its vices defile, nor its errors delude me. May I feel that I am a stranger and a pilgrim on earth, declaring plainly that I seek a country, my title to it becoming daily clearer, my meetness for it more perfect, my foretastes of it more abundant; and, whatsoever I do, may it be done in the Savior's name. Amen.   *Valley of Vision*[30]

Prayer of Illumination

Almighty God, I earnestly ask you for such deeper fellowship of the Holy Spirit, who speaks in the blessed Scriptures, that, when I open them, I may perceive his mind in what I read and immediately hear in them his voice to myself. I ask you for a quicker understanding in spiritual things, for more desire to understand, for a fuller perception of your promise in the church, that I may become teachable and may love that by which you will teach me. Amen.   *Henry Wotherspoon*

⋅ ⋅ ⋅

Scripture Reading

And calling the crowd to him with his disciples, he said to them, "If anyone would come after me, let him deny himself and take up his cross and follow me. For whoever would save his life will lose it, but whoever loses his life for my sake and the gospel's will save it. For what does it profit a man to gain the whole world and forfeit his soul? For what can a man give in return for his soul? For whoever is ashamed of me and of my words in this adulterous and sinful generation, of him will the Son of Man also be ashamed when he comes in the glory of his Father with the holy angels."

And he said to them, "Truly, I say to you, there are some standing here who will not taste death until they see the kingdom of God after it has come with power."   Mark 8:34–9:1

Concise Commentary

With Jesus's three predictions of his sufferings and death in Mark (Mark 8:31; 9:30–31; 10:33–34) he teaches his disciples that the Christ must be *crucified*. Here in Mark 8:34–9:1, with his call to discipleship, he teaches that Christians must be *cruciformed*. That is, Christian discipleship conforms to the pattern of Christ's passion—self-denial and suffering. We must acknowledge both his cross and *ours*: "If anyone would come after me, let him deny himself and take up *his cross* and follow me" (8:34). We can note the structure of this sentence:

> come after me
>> deny himself
>> take up his cross
> follow me

The movements after Jesus ("come after me," which parallels "follow me") flank the admonitions to "deny" oneself and to "take up" one's "cross." I take those four admonitions as parallel thoughts. In other words, the cross is a metaphorical way of speaking of self-denial, and so, in order to "come after" or "follow" Jesus (to be his disciple), we must deny ourselves. From that high calling to lowliness Jesus provides in the following verses a few motivations, all tied to something bigger than us and beyond us—but yet for us. We are to live cruciformed lives because it will go well for us on judgment day, the day when Jesus "comes in the glory of his Father with the holy angels" (8:38). We can think of it this way: if we choose the cross now (lose your life) we get the crown then (save your life), but, if we choose the crown now (gain the whole world), we get the cross then (forfeit your soul). If we are ashamed of Christ—his words and ways—in this life, he will be ashamed of us in the next. Indeed, on judgment day we shall see that the first shall be last and the last first, that to live for self is to die and to die to self is to live, and that the crucified Christ, who rose again, will return in glory with crowns of righteousness for "all who have loved his appearing" (2 Tim. 4:8) and all who have lived for him and others more than for themselves.[31]

Take time to ask God, through his Spirit, to remind you, as the Heidelberg Catechism puts it, that you "belong, body and soul . . . not to [your]self but to [your] faithful Savior Jesus Christ," and thus, if you are to follow a crucified Christ, you must live a cruciformed life. Also ask that God would help you to persevere in the holy habit of self-denial.

Memory Verse

Since then we have a great high priest who has passed through the heavens, Jesus, the Son of God, let us hold fast our confession. *Hebrews 4:14*

· · ·

"Take My Life"
Frances R. Havergal · *1874*

Take my life and let it be
consecrated, Lord, to thee.
Take my moments and my days;
let them flow in endless praise,
let them flow in endless praise.

Take my hands and let them move
at the impulse of thy love.
Take my feet and let them be
swift and beautiful for thee,
swift and beautiful for thee.

Take my voice and let me sing
always, only, for my King.

Take my lips and let them be
filled with messages from thee,
filled with messages from thee.

Take my silver and my gold;
not a mite would I withhold.
Take my intellect and use
every power as thou shalt choose,
every power as thou shalt choose.

Take my will and make it thine;
it shall be no longer mine.
Take my heart it is thine own;
it shall be thy royal throne,
it shall be thy royal throne.

Take my love; my Lord, I pour
at thy feet its treasure store.
Take myself, and I will be
ever, only, all for thee,
ever, only, all for thee.

Perseverance

Part 3 of 5

Adoration

Pray the prayer below. Then pause to praise God for who he is and what he has done.

Lord, I join with Moses, Miriam, and the people of Israel after you delivered them from Pharoah and his army, and I praise you for my salvation in Christ, saying:

I will sing to the LORD, for he has triumphed gloriously;
    the horse and his rider he has thrown into the sea.
The LORD is my strength and my song,
    and he has become my salvation;
this is my God, and I will praise him,
    my father's God, and I will exalt him.
The LORD is a man of war;
    the LORD is his name.

Your right hand, O LORD, glorious in power,
    your right hand, O LORD, shatters the enemy.
In the greatness of your majesty you overthrow your adversaries;
    you send out your fury; it consumes them like stubble.

Who is like you, O LORD, among the gods?
    Who is like you, majestic in holiness,
    awesome in glorious deeds, doing wonders?

You stretched out your right hand;
the earth swallowed them.
You have led in your steadfast love the people whom you have
redeemed;
you have guided them by your strength to your holy abode.
The LORD will reign forever and ever.
Exodus 15:1–3, 6–7, 11–13, 18

Confession
Pray the prayer below. Then take time to ask God through Jesus to forgive specific sins.

Behold, Lord, I am an empty vessel that needs to be filled. My Lord, fill it. I am weak in the faith; strengthen me. I am cold in love; warm me and make me fervent, that my love may go out to my neighbor. I do not have a strong and firm faith; at times I doubt and am unable to trust you altogether. O Lord, help me. Strengthen my faith and my trust in you. In you I have sealed the treasure of all I have. I am poor; you are rich and came to be merciful to the poor. I am a sinner; you are upright. With me there is an abundance of sin; in you is the fullness of righteousness. Therefore, I will remain with you, for who else offers the forgiveness of all my evil attitudes and actions? Who else has the words of eternal life? Amen.
Martin Luther

Thanksgiving
Thank God for the truth that "If we confess our sins, he is faithful and just to forgive us our sins and to cleanse us from all unrighteousness" (1 John 1:9), then pray the prayer below. Finally, take time to thank God for specific blessings in your life. Also feel free to offer Psalm 118:1 ("Oh give thanks to the LORD, for he is good; for his steadfast love endures forever!") as a repeated refrain as you list off (and lift up!) to God people, events, gifts, and circumstances for which you are thankful.

O Lord, from the bottom of my heart I thank you for all your blessings that you have bestowed on my soul and my body, for electing me in your love, redeeming me by your Son, sanctifying me by your Spirit, and preserving me until this present day and hour, by your most gracious providence. Amen.   Lewis Bayly

Supplication
After you pray the prayer below, feel free to add your own specific requests.

Holy Spirit, draw my heart from darkness to light. Show me the glory of my Redeemer; cause me to revel in his love and to bask in the joy of his great pleasure in me. Enable me to hate the darkness of my sin and to flee to the brightness of his love, which welcomes me as a treasured child reclothed in the brightness of his obedience. Help me to live not for my own glory but for the glory of Jesus—the one who gave himself to redeem me. Prepare me for the day when I will fall at Jesus' feet and live in the bright light of his glory in my heavenly home forever. Amen.   *Barbara R. Duguid*[32]

Prayer of Illumination
Lord, send your Spirit forth at this time upon me and by him keep me, that I may ever render up the fruits of the Holy Ghost: love, joy, peace, patience, gentleness, goodness, faith, meekness, and self-control. Amen.   *Cyril of Jerusalem*

• • •

Scripture Reading
"Simon, Simon, behold, Satan demanded to have you, that he might sift you like wheat, but I have prayed for you that your faith may not fail. And when you have turned again, strengthen your brothers." Peter said to him, "Lord, I am ready to go with you both to prison and to death." Jesus said, "I tell you, Peter, the rooster will not crow this day, until you deny three times that you know me." . . .

Then they seized him [Jesus] and led him away, bringing him into the high priest's house, and Peter was following at a distance. And when they had kindled a fire in the middle of the courtyard and sat down together, Peter sat down among them. Then a servant girl, seeing him as he sat in the light and looking closely at him, said, "This man also was with him." But he denied it, saying, "Woman, I do not know him." And a little later someone else saw him and said, "You also are one of them." But Peter said, "Man, I am not." And after an interval of about an hour still another insisted, saying, "Certainly this man also was with him, for he too is a Galilean." But Peter said, "Man, I do not know what you are talking about." And immediately, while he was still speaking, the rooster crowed. And the Lord turned and looked at Peter. And Peter remembered the saying of the Lord, how he had said to him, "Before the rooster crows today, you will deny me three times." And he went out and wept bitterly.   *Luke 22:31–34, 54–62*

Concise Commentary

Notice the irony. While Jesus stands strong and composed in the middle of evil opposition from Israel's leading men, Peter cowardly collapses under a few simple questions from a servant girl and some bystanders. While Jesus is being slapped and spit upon and mocked as a false prophet, his prophecy about Peter is fulfilled! Learn also four lessons. First, we should take Proverbs 16:18 to heart: "Pride goes before destruction, and a haughty spirit before a fall." At the Last Supper Peter boasts in his bravery and resilience: "Even though they all fall away, I will not" (Mark 14:29). What a sad line. In one packed-with-pride pronouncement he contradicts Jesus, is condescending toward his friends, and is overly self-confident. Then, a short time later, they all are emphatic about their allegiance to Jesus, but it is Peter who is the first to say, "If I must die with you, I will not deny you" (14:31). Watch out for pride. It is Peter's downfall here; it can be our undoing as well. Second, Luke's candid retelling of Peter's personal testimony of temporary apostasy clearly teaches us the absolute need for Jesus's atoning death. Peter might have come to Caiaphas's palace because he hoped to save Jesus, but that very night he would learn what he would preach till his death: "There is salvation in *no one else*, for there is *no other name* under heaven given among men by which we must be saved" (Acts 4:12).

Third, we need Jesus not only for our salvation but also for our perseverance in the faith. The only reason that Satan does not sift Simon Peter like chaff thrown into the fire is because Jesus prays ("But I have prayed for you that your faith may not fail," Luke 22:32). Without Jesus's prayer for us—his intercession now in heaven—we are without hope of finishing the race. Fourth, Jesus not only forgives Peter of this hideous sin; he restores him to fellowship with both God and the church, and he even uses him to encourage others ("And when you have returned again [repented], strengthen your brothers," 22:32). In Acts we read of his amazing words of encouragement and evangelism! "Filled with the Holy Spirit," Peter spoke "the word of God with boldness" (Acts 4:31).[33]

Prayer Prompt
Take time to thank God that he is a forgiving God. Thank him also that he is a God who restores relationships and empowers even great sinners who repent to accomplish great things for his glory. If you have denied Jesus, come back to him now. Repent, renew your relationship with God, and ask the Father to fill you with the Spirit so you might boldly proclaim the gospel of Jesus Christ.

Memory Verse
Since then we have a great high priest who has passed through the heavens, Jesus, the Son of God, let us hold fast our confession.
Hebrews 4:14

. . .

"Abide with Me"
Henry Francis Lyte · 1847

Abide with me: fast falls the eventide;
the darkness deepens; Lord, with me abide.
When other helpers fail and comforts flee,
Help of the helpless, O abide with me.

Swift to its close ebbs out life's little day;
Earth's joys grow dim, its glories pass away.
Change and decay in all around I see.
O thou who changest not, abide with me.

I need thy presence every passing hour.
What but thy grace can foil the tempter's pow'r?
Who like thyself my guide and strength can be?
Through cloud and sunshine, O abide with me.

I fear no foe with thee at hand to bless,
ills have no weight, and tears no bitterness.
Where is death's sting? Where, grave, thy victory?
I triumph still, if thou abide with me.

Hold thou thy cross before my closing eyes.
Shine through the gloom and point me to the skies.
Heav'n's morning breaks and earth's vain shadows flee;
in life, in death, O Lord, abide with me.

34

Perseverance

Part 4 of 5

Adoration
Pray the prayer below. Then pause to praise God for who he is and what he has done.

I cry out with a loud voice and praise you, O Lord God, who are from everlasting to everlasting. You are the Lord, and you alone. You have made heaven, the heaven of heavens, with all their host, the earth and all that is on it, the seas and all that is in them; and you preserve all of them; and the host of heaven worships you. You are the Lord, the God who chose Abram from among the nations to bless through his offspring (our Lord Jesus) people from all the nations. You are so righteous and gracious! You are the Lord, the God who saw the affliction and heard the cries of your people when they were slaves in Egypt. You delivered them from Pharoah and his armies, led them in the wilderness with a pillar of cloud by day and a pillar of fire by night, gave them your right rules and true laws, gave them your good Spirit to instruct them, provided bread from heaven and water from the rock, and safely brought them into the promised land, a land where they ate and were satisfied and delighted themselves in your great goodness. Through Christ you delivered us from the sin and judgment we deserved, you have written the law of love in our hearts through the Holy Spirit, you daily lead and

guide and provide and protect, and soon you will take us to heaven, to paradise regained. O Bread of Heaven, I praise you!
Based on Nehemiah 9

Confession
Pray the prayer below. Then take time to ask God through Jesus to forgive specific sins.

Lord, God, remembering the dreadful judgment hanging over our heads, and always ready to fall upon us, let me return unto you with all contrition and meekness of heart, bewailing and lamenting my sinful life, acknowledging and confessing my offenses, and seeking to bring forth worthy fruits of repentance. For now is the axe put unto the root of the trees, so that every tree that bringeth not forth good fruit is hewn down, and cast into the fire. Let me not abuse the goodness of God, who calls us mercifully to amendment, and of his endless pity promises us forgiveness of that which is past, if with a perfect and true heart we return unto him. For though our sins be as red as scarlet, they shall be made white as snow; and though they be like purple, yet they shall be made white as wool. Although I have sinned, yet I have an Advocate with the Father, Jesus Christ the righteous; and he is the propitiation for our sins. For he was wounded for our offences, and smitten for our wickedness. Amen.
Book of Common Prayer (1662)

Thanksgiving
Thank God for the truth that "If we confess our sins, he is faithful and just to forgive us our sins and to cleanse us from all unrighteousness" (1 John 1:9), then pray the prayer below. Finally, take time to thank God for specific blessings in your life. Also feel free to offer Psalm 118:1 ("Oh give thanks to the Lord, *for he is good; for his steadfast love endures forever!") as a repeated refrain as you list off (and lift up!) to God people, events, gifts, and circumstances for which you are thankful.*

My heart is steadfast, O God!
    I will sing and make melody with all my being!
Awake, O harp and lyre!
    I will awake the dawn!
I will give thanks to you, O Lord, among the peoples;
    I will sing praises to you among the nations.
For your steadfast love is great above the heavens;
    your faithfulness reaches to the clouds.

Be exalted, O God, above the heavens!
    Let your glory be over all the earth!
That your beloved ones may be delivered,
    give salvation by your right hand and answer me!
    Psalm 108:1–6

Supplication
After you pray the prayer below, feel free to add your own specific requests.

When the storms of life are raging, stand by me. When the world
is tossing me like a ship upon the sea, you who rule the wind and
waves, stand by me. In the midst of tribulation, stand by me;
When the hosts of hell assail, and my strength begins to fail, you
who never lost a battle, stand by me. In the midst of faults and
failures, stand by me. When I do the best I can, and my friends
misunderstand, you who know everything about me, stand by
me. In the midst of persecution, stand by me. When my foes in
battle array undertake to stop my way, you who saved Paul and
Silas, stand by me. When I am growing old and feeble, stand by
me. When my life becomes a burden, and I am nearing chilly
Jordan, O stand by me. Amen.   *Charles Albert Tindley*

Prayer of Illumination
Lord of Life, you said to Lazarus, "Come forth," and he came to
life. Breathe your Spirit on me now, that your living word may

come alive to me. Light of the World, you said to the deaf man, "Be opened," and his ears could hear. Open my ears to hear your voice through your sacred Scriptures. Son of David, you promised to lead the blind; not only lead me, but open my eyes so I might know how to follow you through knowing, loving, and heeding all your commands. Amen.

◆ ◆ ◆

Scripture Reading

I [Paul] have fought the good fight, I have finished the race, I have kept the faith. Henceforth there is laid up for me the crown of righteousness, which the Lord, the righteous judge, will award to me on that day, and not only to me but also to all who have loved his appearing.

Do your best [Timothy] to come to me soon. For Demas, in love with this present world, has deserted me and gone to Thessalonica. Crescens has gone to Galatia, Titus to Dalmatia. Luke alone is with me. Get Mark and bring him with you, for he is very useful to me for ministry. Tychicus I have sent to Ephesus. When you come, bring the cloak that I left with Carpus at Troas, also the books, and above all the parchments. Alexander the coppersmith did me great harm; the Lord will repay him according to his deeds. Beware of him yourself, for he strongly opposed our message. At my first defense no one came to stand by me, but all deserted me. May it not be charged against them! But the Lord stood by me and strengthened me, so that through me the message might be fully proclaimed and all the Gentiles might hear it. So I was rescued from the lion's mouth. The Lord will rescue me from every evil deed and bring me safely into his heavenly kingdom. To him be the glory forever and ever. Amen.

Greet Prisca and Aquila, and the household of Onesiphorus. Erastus remained at Corinth, and I left Trophimus, who was ill, at Miletus. Do your best to come before winter. Eubulus sends greetings to you, as do Pudens and Linus and Claudia and all the brothers. The Lord be with your spirit. Grace be with you.

2 Timothy 4:7–22

Concise Commentary

Paul concludes his second letter to Timothy by charging him to "preach the word," that is, to "do the work of an evangelist" (2 Tim. 4:2, 5) and preach faithfully the good news about Jesus from the Bible (see 3:15). He exhorts him to finish well, as Paul himself has ("I have fought the good fight, I have finished the race, I have kept the faith," 4:7). He also invites (strongly encourages!) Timothy to visit him in prison before Paul dies: "Do your best to come to me soon" (4:9; cf. 4:21). But there is more to that clear command. Did you notice all the names? Seventeen! As with the lists of names in the Bible's genealogies, which you perhaps skip or skim, you might not make much of these names. But notice a few important details. First and most obvious, these names remind us that the church is composed of people. Second, the church then and now is made up of both Jews and Gentiles and men and women from around the world, e.g., Galatia (Turkey), Corinth (Greece), and Dalmatia (Croatia). Moreover, the Latin (Prisca, Aquila, Pudens, Linus, Claudia) and Greek (Onesiphorus, Erastus, Trophimus, Eubulus) names remind us of the success of Jesus's prediction that the gospel would spread "to the end of the earth" (Acts 1:8). Here Paul rejoices that "through me the message might be fully proclaimed and all the Gentiles might hear it" (2 Tim. 4:17).

Third, notice that Paul names not only members of the church but apostates (Demas) and enemies (Alexander) as well; in doing so he reminds both Timothy and us that it is dangerous to follow Jesus, and he reminds the church of the need to endure through betrayals, trials, temptations, and persecutions. Paul makes clear that God has not left us to fight the good fight alone! Paul mentions two divinely ordained ways by which God helps us keep the faith: faithful friends and our loving Savior.

The present companionship of Luke ("Luke alone is with me") and future companionship of Timothy and Mark ("Get Mark and bring him with you," 2:11), Paul believes, will sustain him till the end. Moreover, and more importantly, he thanks Jesus for his faithfulness in the past ("The Lord stood by me and strengthened me," 4:17) and trusts that he will bring him safely home ("The Lord will rescue me from every evil deed and bring me safely into his heavenly kingdom," 4:18). We should believe the same, and we should praise our Lord for such a salvation: "To him be the glory forever and ever. Amen" (4:18).

Prayer Prompt
Take time to thank God for the "sacred writings, which are able to make you wise for salvation through faith in Christ Jesus." And ask him now to take what you learned today from the end of Paul's epistle ("All Scripture is breathed out by God"!) to teach, reprove, correct, and train you in righteousness and to equip you for every good work (see 2 Tim. 3:15–17).

Memory Verse
Since then we have a great high priest who has passed through the heavens, Jesus, the Son of God, let us hold fast our confession.
Hebrews 4:14

. . .

"For All the Saints"
William Walsham How · 1864

For all the saints who from their labors rest,
who Thee by faith before the world confessed;

Thy name, O Jesus, be forever blest.
Alleluia, Alleluia!

Thou wast their Rock, their Fortress and their Might;
Thou, Lord, their Captain in the well-fought fight;
Thou, in the darkness drear, their one true Light.
Alleluia, Alleluia!

O blest communion, fellowship divine!
We feebly struggle; they in glory shine;
yet all are one in Thee, for all are Thine.
Alleluia, Alleluia!

And when the strife is fierce, the warfare long,
steals on the ear the distant triumph song,
and hearts are brave again, and arms are strong.
Alleluia, Alleluia!

But then there breaks a still more glorious day;
The saints triumphant rise in bright array;
The King of glory passes on His way,
Alleluia, Alleluia!

From earth's wide bounds, from ocean's farthest coast,
Through gates of pearl streams in the countless host,
Singing to Father, Son, and Holy Ghost,
Alleluia, Alleluia!

Perseverance

Part 5 of 5

Adoration
Pray the prayer below. Then pause to praise God for who he is and what he has done.

One thing have I asked of the LORD,
    that will I seek after:
that I may dwell in the house of the LORD
    all the days of my life,
to gaze upon the beauty of the LORD
    and to inquire in his temple.   *Psalm 27:4*

O Lord Jesus, I long for the day when I "will see [your] face" (Rev. 22:4) and live forever in your presence.

Confession
Pray the prayer below. Then take time to ask God through Jesus to forgive specific sins.

O Lord, I bless you, not only for the pardon of those sins I have committed but also for your goodness in preserving me from many thousands I was prone to fall into, which is in effect, the pardon of so many. I pray not only for my sins today but tomorrow and the next year. Amen.   *Anthony Burgess*

Thanksgiving

Thank God for the truth that "If we confess our sins, he is faithful and just to forgive us our sins and to cleanse us from all unrighteousness" (1 John 1:9), then pray the prayer below. Finally, take time to thank God for specific blessings in your life. Also feel free to offer Psalm 118:1 ("Oh give thanks to the LORD, for he is good; for his steadfast love endures forever!") as a repeated refrain as you list off (and lift up!) to God people, events, gifts, and circumstances for which you are thankful.

All-sufficient King, when I come into your presence, I see the glory of your perfections, the throne of your eternal and universal kingdom, the ten thousand times ten thousand angels who minister to you. Impress on my mind the consciousness of your greatness, not to drive me from you but to inspire me to approach you; not to diminish my confidence in you but to lead me to admire your great condescension. You have been mindful of me and visited me, taken charge of me from birth, cared for me in all conditions for me, fed me at your table, drawn the curtains of love around me, and given me new mercies every morning. Thank you! Amen.   *Valley of Vision*[34]

Supplication

After you pray the prayer below, feel free to add your own specific requests.

Bring me, O Lord God, at my last awakening into the house and gate of heaven, to enter into that gate and dwell in that house where there will be no darkness nor dazzling but one equal light; no noise nor silence but one equal music; no fear nor hopes but one equal possession; no ends nor beginnings but one equal eternity in the presence of your glory and dominion, world without end. Amen.   Daily Prayer[35]

Prayer of Illumination

I pray that you would circumcise my ears and heart to hear, love, and receive with meekness the word. Make me good soil

to receive the good seed of the word, and strengthen me against the temptations of Satan, the cares of the world, the hardness of my own heart, and whatever may hinder me from hearing your voice. I pray that Christ may be so formed in me, and live in me, that all my thoughts may be brought into captivity to him and my heart established in every good work forever. Amen.
The Westminster Assembly

• • •

Scripture Reading
> The LORD is my shepherd; I shall not want.
>> He makes me lie down in green pastures.
>> He leads me beside still waters.
>> He restores my soul.
> He leads me in paths of righteousness
>> for his name's sake.
>
> Even though I walk through the valley of the shadow of death,
>> I will fear no evil,
> for you are with me;
>> your rod and your staff,
>> they comfort me.
>
> You prepare a table before me
>> in the presence of my enemies;
> you anoint my head with oil;
>> my cup overflows.
> Surely goodness and mercy shall follow me
>> all the days of my life,
> and I shall dwell in the house of the LORD
>> forever.   *Psalm 23*

Psalm 23 is a song that uses simple pastoral words and images. Because of this we often fail to recognize its poetic brilliance and theological depth. Here are four details to observe, appreciate, and apply. First, the psalm is structured around six characters and three personal confessions: sheep and shepherd, verses 1–3 ("I shall not want"); traveler and companion, verse 4 ("I shall not fear"), and guest and host, verses 5–6 ("I shall dwell").[36] Of course the sheep, traveler, and guest symbolize believers, and the shepherd, companion, and host represent God. Second, the "God" of Psalm 23 is the covenant God of Israel, the great I Am Who I Am (*Yahweh*, which is often rendered as "LORD"). What is amazing is that the Lord of the universe cares personally for each believer: "The Lord is *my* shepherd." And this reality is expressed not just at the start of the poem but throughout. Notice "the Lord-I," "he-me," and "you-me" language found in each line. Moreover, notice how our God draws closer to us through the deepest darkness of our lives and how the poem expresses this intimacy with the transition from "he-me" to "you-me," from "He leads me in the paths of righteousness" to "Even though I walk through the valley of the shadow of death, I will fear no evil, for you are with me."

Third, notice that in much of this poem we are passive and needy (we require food, water, rest, guidance, shelter, comfort, housing, and help), while God is active: he makes, leads, restores, prepares, and anoints.[37] David Gibson voices this truth beautifully: "The self-sufficient God is not the self-absorbed God. The self-existent God is not the self-centered God. Rather—wonder of wonders—the God who is so strong clothes himself in a picture [that of a good shepherd, but we could include closest companion and generous host] of the closest tender care for those who are so weak."[38] Fourth, the ultimate embodiment of such tender care came in the incarnation, when our "Good Shepherd"

Jesus laid "down his life for the sheep" (John 10:11). Through his death he takes away our sins so we can be forgiven, and, because we are forgiven, we can dwell in the presence of God forever.

Prayer Prompt

Take time to ask God, through his Spirit, to help you to "behold the Lamb of God, who takes away the sin of the world!" (John 1:29). And ask that you would be able to express the total trust in your Good Shepherd that David expresses in Psalm 23. Place all your wants and worries, and dark days and fearful thoughts, into the care of a God who is "with" you ("You are with me," 23:4)[39] and thus a God who will provide and protect you both now and forever.

> Memory Verse
>
> Since then we have a great high priest who has passed through the heavens, Jesus, the Son of God, let us hold fast our confession. (Hebrews 4:14)

♦ ♦ ♦

"The King of Love My Shepherd Is"
H. W. Baker • 1868[40]

The King of love my shepherd is,
whose goodness faileth never.
I nothing lack if I am his,
and he is mine forever.

Where streams of living water flow,
my ransomed soul he leadeth;

and where the verdant pastures grow,
with food celestial feedeth.

Perverse and foolish, oft I strayed,
but yet in love he sought me;
and on his shoulder gently laid,
and home, rejoicing, brought me.

In death's dark vale I fear no ill,
with thee, dear Lord, beside me;
thy rod and staff my comfort still,
thy cross before to guide me.

Thou spreadst a table in my sight;
thy unction grace bestoweth;
and oh, what transport of delight
from thy pure chalice floweth!

And so through all the length of days,
thy goodness faileth never;
Good Shepherd, may I sing thy praise
within thy house forever.

Witness

Part 1 of 5

Through these biblical and ancient Christian prayers offer your adoration and gratitude to God, confess your sins, and ask for help to read his word and live the Christian life. If it helps, pray aloud and with physical gestures, such as raising your hands (1 Tim. 2:8) when you praise God's holy name or kneeling (Dan. 6:10) or lying prostrate (Luke 5:8) when you confess your sins. Using different postures to pray can engage your body and mind in new ways! "Stand up and bless the LORD your God from everlasting to everlasting" (Neh. 9:5).

Gloria Patri
Pray the Gloria Patri. Then take time to praise and thank God for specific blessings in your life.

Glory be to the Father, and to the Son, and to the Holy Ghost,
As it was in the beginning, is now, and ever shall be,
    world without end.
Amen.

Agnus Dei
Pray the Agnus Dei. Then take time to ask God through Jesus to forgive specific sins. Also offer prayers of lament. Pray that God would deal with sufferings and injustices both now and when Christ returns. Cry out, "O Sovereign

Lord, holy and true, how long before you will judge and avenge our blood on those who dwell on the earth?" (Rev. 6:10), or "Out of the depths I cry to you, O LORD! O Lord, hear my voice! Let your ears be attentive to the voice of my pleas for mercy!" (Ps. 130:1–2).

Lamb of God, who takes away the sins of the world,
    have mercy on us.
Lamb of God, who takes away the sins of the world,
    have mercy on us.
Lamb of God, who takes away the sins of the world,
    grant us peace. Amen.

The Lord's Prayer
Pray each line slowly. As you think about each petition, add your own specific requests.

Our Father in heaven,
hallowed be your name.
Your kingdom come,
your will be done,
    on earth as it is in heaven.
Give us this day our daily bread,
and forgive us our debts,
    as we also have forgiven our debtors.
And lead us not into temptation,
    but deliver us from evil.   Matthew 6:9–13

Prayer of Illumination
Have pity, O Lord, upon my weakness, and give me a sharper mind to understand the true sense of your word, a simplicity of heart to receive it, an integrity to declare it, and a zeal to instill it in others and defend it. Amen.   Philip Doddridge

• • •

Scripture Reading

> [Lord], I am continually with you;
>> you hold my right hand.
> You guide me with your counsel,
>> and afterward you will receive me to glory.
> Whom have I in heaven but you?
>> And there is nothing on earth that I desire besides you.
> My flesh and my heart may fail,
>> but God is the strength of my heart and my portion forever.
>
> For behold, those who are far from you shall perish;
>> you put an end to everyone who is unfaithful to you.
> But for me it is good to be near God;
>> I have made the Lord God my refuge,
>> that I may tell of all your works.   Psalm 73:23–28

Concise Commentary

Psalm 73 ends on a very different note than it begins. In verses 1–22 the psalmist acknowledges that God is good ("Truly God is good," 73:1), yet he cannot understand why God allows the righteous to suffer and the wicked to prosper. The psalmist knows well from Scripture that God justly governs the whole world and that God particularly cares for his people, but he struggles with the reality that what is clear to the eye of faith is blurred by his experience. God seems to be punishing the righteous and the humble but blessing the wicked and the proud. The psalmist honestly admits that, because of this, he is tempted to envy the evil and arrogant and that his temptation has pushed him to the edge of his convictions. He has nearly slipped into apostasy (leaving God and following the ways of the world). His eyes are fixed only on what he sees in the here and now. It is not until he "went into the sanctuary of God" (73:17, the temple) that his perspective changed. Perhaps this happens to you too! After a difficult week in the world, you come to church on Sunday, gather with God's people, hear from God's word, are retold the story of Christ's sacrifice, and are reminded, as is the psalmist, that there are two ways to live and two final destinations.

Those who ignore God and live by their own rules may not be judged in this lifetime, but they will be judged soon enough; they will "fall to ruin" and be "destroyed in a moment, swept away utterly by terrors!" (73:18, 19); "For behold, those who are far from you shall perish; you put an end to everyone who is unfaithful to you" (73:27). This is the "end" (literally "the afterward," 73:17) of the wicked. But the godly, who remain faithful to our faithful God through all the trials and temptations this world has to offer, will be rewarded with glory ("You will receive me to glory," 73:24). This reminder of God's revelation turns the psalmist Godward. Now, at the end of the poem, all he wants and needs is God ("There is nothing on earth that I desire besides you," 73:25; "God is the strength of my heart and my portion forever," 73:26; "I have made the Lord GOD my refuge," 73:28). This reminder of God's revelation also turns him outward: "I have made the Lord GOD my refuge, that I may tell of all your works" (73:28). Spiritual intimacy with God creates, in the psalmist, evangelistic zeal for others. He wants everyone to know God. So he declares that he will declare the good news of God to others as long as he lives. Let us follow in his steps.

Prayer Prompt
Take time to ask God, through his Spirit, to renew your vision of him so that you might trust him through the trials of life and share the good news of salvation with others, inviting them to join you in worshiping our good and faithful and just God.

• • •

"A Mighty Fortress Is Our God"
Martin Luther · 1529

A mighty fortress is our God,
a bulwark never failing;
our helper He, amid the flood
of mortal ills prevailing.
For still our ancient foe
doth seek to work us woe;
his craft and power are great,
and armed with cruel hate,
on earth is not his equal.

Did we in our own strength confide,
our striving would be losing,
were not the right Man on our side,
the Man of God's own choosing.
Dost ask who that may be?
Christ Jesus, it is He;
Lord Sabaoth His name,
from age to age the same;
and He must win the battle.

And though this world, with devils filled,
should threaten to undo us,
we will not fear, for God hath willed
His truth to triumph through us.
The prince of darkness grim,
we tremble not for him;
his rage we can endure,
for lo! his doom is sure;
one little word shall fell him.

That Word above all earthly powers
no thanks to them abideth;
the Spirit and the gifts are ours
through Him who with us sideth.
Let goods and kindred go,
this mortal life also;
the body they may kill:
God's truth abideth still;
His kingdom is forever!

Witness

Part 2 of 5

Adoration

Pray the prayer below. Then pause to praise God for who he is and what he has done.

Bless the LORD, O my soul,
    and all that is within me,
    bless his holy name!
Bless the LORD, O my soul,
    and forget not all his benefits,
who forgives all your iniquity,
    who heals all your diseases,
who redeems your life from the pit,
    who crowns you with steadfast love and mercy,
who satisfies you with good
    so that your youth is renewed like the eagle's.   Psalm 103:1–5

Confession

Pray the prayer below. Then take time to ask God through Jesus to forgive specific sins.

Father, I plead Jesus's blood to pay my debts of wrong. Accept his worthiness for my unworthiness, his sinlessness for my transgressions, his purity for my uncleanness, his sincerity for my guile, his truth for my deceits, his meekness for my pride, his constancy for my backslidings, his love for my enmity, his fullness for my emptiness, his faithfulness for my treachery, his obedience for my lawlessness, his glory for my shame, his devotedness for my waywardness, his holy life for my unchaste ways, his righteousness for my dead works, his death for my life. Amen.　　*Valley of Vision*[41]

Thanksgiving

Thank God for the truth that "If we confess our sins, he is faithful and just to forgive us our sins and to cleanse us from all unrighteousness" (1 John 1:9), then pray the prayer below. Finally, take time to thank God for specific blessings in your life. Also feel free to offer Psalm 118:1 ("Oh give thanks to the LORD, *for he is good; for his steadfast love endures forever!") as a repeated refrain as you list off (and lift up!) to God people, events, gifts, and circumstances for which you are thankful.*

Blessed are you, O LORD, the God of Israel our father, forever and ever. Yours, O LORD, is the greatness and the power and the glory and the victory and the majesty, for all that is in the heavens and in the earth is yours. Yours is the kingdom, O LORD, and you are exalted as head above all. Both riches and honor come from you, and you rule over all. In your hand are power and might, and in your hand it is to make great and to give strength to all. And now [I] thank you, [my] God, and praise your glorious name.　　1 Chronicles 29:10–13

Supplication

After you pray the prayer below, feel free to add your own specific requests.

Set your fear before my eyes, and let your Spirit so rule my heart that all I shall think, do, or speak this day may tend to your glory, the good of others, and the peace of my own conscience. And to this end I commend myself, and all my ways and actions, together with all that belong to me, to your gracious direction and protection. I pray that you would keep both them and me from all evil, and to give a blessing to all my honest labors and endeavors. Defend your whole church. Preserve the governing authorities of our country. Bless all our church leaders. Be favorable to all who fear you and tremble at your judgments. Comfort all those that are sick and comfortless. Lord, keep me in a continual readiness, by faith and repentance, for my last end, that whether I live or die, I may be found your own, to your eternal glory and my everlasting salvation, through Jesus Christ my only Savior, in whose blessed name I beg these mercies at your hands and give to you your praise and glory. Amen.   *Lewis Bayly*

Prayer of Illumination
O God, as I read your word, search the deepest recesses of my heart; try me and expose my anxious thoughts and inmost concerns. Help me to see my sins and lead me in the path to everlasting life! Amen.   *Based on Psalm 119:23–24*

• • •

Scripture Reading
He entered Jericho and was passing through. And behold, there was a man named Zacchaeus. He was a chief tax collector and was rich. And he was seeking to see who Jesus was, but on account of the crowd he could not, because he was small in stature. So he ran on ahead and climbed up into a sycamore tree to see him, for he was about to pass that way. And when Jesus came to the place, he looked up and said to him, "Zacchaeus, hurry and come down, for I must stay at your house today." So he hurried and came down and received him joyfully. And when they saw it, they all grumbled, "He has gone in to be the guest of a man who is a sinner." And Zacchaeus stood and said to the Lord, "Behold, Lord, the half of my goods I give to the poor. And if I have defrauded anyone

of anything, I restore it fourfold." And Jesus said to him, "Today salvation has come to this house, since he also is a son of Abraham. For the Son of Man came to seek and to save the lost."   *Luke 19:1–10*

Concise Commentary

Three words can be used to tell Zacchaeus's salvation story: seeking, receiving, and pulling. We are told that Zacchaeus "was *seeking* to see who Jesus was" (Luke 19:3). But we are also told that "he was a chief tax collector and was rich" (19:2), as well as "small in stature" (19:3). The first two details tell us that he was filthy rich, as Jewish tax collectors collected money from the Jews on behalf of the Romans, overcharged people, and kept the difference. Zacchaeus was a traitor and a thief. The third detail—regarding his height—sets up the story. While he was seeking Jesus, he could not see Jesus over the crowd. So he came up with a solution to his "small" problem. He ran ahead of the crowd and climbed into a sycamore tree. Now he could see Jesus as Jesus walked by. But, interestingly, Luke records that it was Jesus who saw him: "He *looked up* and said to him, 'Zacchaeus, hurry and come down, for I must stay at your house today." Sure enough, Zacchaeus obeyed. He hurried down the tree "and received him joyfully" (19:5–6). *Receiving!* He received Jesus with his emotions ("joyfully") and, later in his house, with his actions of repentance and faith: "Lord, half of what I have, I give the poor. And all the people I have cheated I will give them back four times as much" (see 19:8). Amazing!

What is more amazing is what Jesus said next: "Today salvation has come to this house" because Zacchaeus believed in Jesus (v. 9). The people grumbled that Jesus had "gone in to be the guest of a man who is a sinner" (19:7), but Zacchaeus knew that Jesus came even for people like him. Here is where the word *pulling* comes into play. The last line in the story, which is the most important, comes from Jesus: "For the Son of Man came to seek and to save the lost" (19:10). Jesus came to save sinners!

But how does that saying relate to the idea of pulling? In 18:25 Jesus had taught, "It is easier for a camel to go through the eye of a needle than for a rich person to enter the kingdom of God" (18:25)? Zacchaeus is rich! So how did he get through the eye? Jesus pulled him through! Jesus came to seek and save the lost—even the filthy rich. All things are possible for God.

Prayer Prompt
Take time to ask God to remind you of the amazing truths that Jesus came to seek and save the lost and that nothing is impossible for God. Pray now for those people in your life who are seeking after Jesus but have not yet received him. Pray also for those who seem farthest away from entering the kingdom of God through faith in Christ. Pray that God would give you the faith to believe that he can do the impossible.

Memory Verse
And Jesus came and said to them, "All authority in heaven and on earth has been given to me. Go therefore and make disciples of all nations, baptizing them in the name of the Father and of the Son and of the Holy Spirit, teaching them to observe all that I have commanded you. And behold, I am with you always, to the end of the age." Matthew 28:18–20

• • •

"I Heard the Voice of Jesus Say"
Horatius Bonar • 1846[42]

I heard the voice of Jesus say,
"Come unto Me and rest;

lay down, thou weary one, lay down
thy head upon My breast."
I came to Jesus as I was,
so weary, worn, and sad;
I found in Him a resting place,
and He has made me glad.

I heard the voice of Jesus say,
"Behold, I freely give
the living water, thirsty one;
stoop down, and drink, and live."
I came to Jesus, and I drank
of that life-giving stream;
my thirst was quenched, my soul revived,
and now I live in Him.

I heard the voice of Jesus say,
"I am this dark world's Light;
look unto Me, thy morn shall rise,
and all thy day be bright."
I looked to Jesus, and I found
in Him my Star, my Sun;
and in that Light of life I'll walk,
till trav'ling days are done.

Witness

Part 3 of 5

Adoration
Pray the prayer below. Then pause to praise God for who he is and what he has done.

I will extol you, my God and King,
    and bless your name forever and ever.
Every day I will bless you
    and praise your name forever and ever.
Great is the LORD, and greatly to be praised,
    and his greatness is unsearchable.

One generation shall commend your works to another,
    and shall declare your mighty acts.
On the glorious splendor of your majesty,
    and on your wondrous works, I will meditate.
They shall speak of the might of your awesome deeds,
    and I will declare your greatness.
They shall pour forth the fame of your abundant goodness
    and shall sing aloud of your righteousness.   *Psalm 145:1–7*

Confession
Pray the prayer below. Then take time to ask God through Jesus to forgive specific sins.

O God, my heavenly Father, I confess that I have grievously sinned against you in many ways; not only by outward transgression but also by secret thoughts and desires, which I cannot fully understand but which are all known to you. I do earnestly repent and am truly sorry for these my offences. In your great goodness have mercy on me, and for the sake of your dear Son Jesus Christ my Lord forgive my sins and graciously help me overcome my weakness. Amen.   *The Common Service Book (1888)*

Thanksgiving
Thank God for the truth that "If we confess our sins, he is faithful and just to forgive us our sins and to cleanse us from all unrighteousness" (1 John 1:9), then pray the prayer below. Finally, take time to thank God for specific blessings in your life. Also feel free to offer Psalm 118:1 ("Oh give thanks to the Lord, *for he is good; for his steadfast love endures forever!") as a repeated refrain as you list off (and lift up!) to God people, events, gifts, and circumstances for which you are thankful.*

Lord, help me to rejoice in you always. Also help me "not to be anxious about anything" but to turn to you in prayer and "with thanksgiving let [my] requests be made known" to you, believing that your peace, "which surpasses all understanding, will guard" my heart and mind "in Christ Jesus." I thank you that through your power and assistance I can "think about" what is true, honorable, just, pure, lovely, commendable, excellent, and worthy of praise.   *Based on Philippians 4:4–8*

Supplication
After you pray the prayer below, feel free to add your own specific requests.

Heavenly Father, you have called me as a Christian to remember to pray for the church and the world and for the ongoing ministry of the gospel, that it might increase and make disciples of all nations. And so, I pray to the Lord. *Lord, hear my prayer.* For those in need—the poor and the hungry, the homeless and the unemployed, the sick and the lonely—that they may receive help in their distress, I pray to the Lord. *Lord, hear my prayer.* For those who do not yet believe, and for all those in spiritual need, that they may find faith, hope, and comfort, I pray to the Lord. *Lord, hear my prayer.* For our nation and for all who govern, that justice and freedom may be preserved for all citizens and that we may dwell in peace, as so to give a greater opportunity for the spread of the gospel, I pray to the Lord. *Lord, hear my prayer.* For the church throughout the world, and especially for the missionaries from my church, help these brothers and sisters to remain faithful to their calling (help them to proclaim the gospel boldly even in the midst of much conflict) and so prove to be the light of Christ among the nations, I pray to the Lord. *Lord, hear my prayer.* Heavenly Father, grant grace to your people to live as faithful followers of Christ the Lord and as worthy witnesses of your gospel. Have mercy on the peoples of the earth, and draw the lost into your gracious kingdom. Amen.

Prayer of Illumination
Enlighten my mind's eye to study your words, to understand your commandments, to do your will, to sing to you in heartfelt adoration, and to praise your most holy name, Father, Son, and Holy Spirit, now and ever, and to the ages of ages. Amen.
Basil of Caesarea

◆ ◆ ◆

Scripture Reading
Now after the Sabbath, toward the dawn of the first day of the week, Mary Magdalene and the other Mary went to see the tomb. And behold, there was a great earthquake, for an angel of the Lord descended from heaven and came and rolled back the stone

and sat on it. His appearance was like lightning, and his clothing white as snow. And for fear of him the guards trembled and became like dead men. But the angel said to the women, "Do not be afraid, for I know that you seek Jesus who was crucified. He is not here, for he has risen, as he said. Come, see the place where he lay. Then go quickly and tell his disciples that he has risen from the dead, and behold, he is going before you to Galilee; there you will see him. See, I have told you." So they departed quickly from the tomb with fear and great joy, and ran to tell his disciples. And behold, Jesus met them and said, "Greetings!" And they came up and took hold of his feet and worshiped him. Then Jesus said to them, "Do not be afraid; go and tell my brothers to go to Galilee, and there they will see me." . . .

Now the eleven disciples went to Galilee, to the mountain to which Jesus had directed them. And when they saw him they worshiped him, but some doubted. And Jesus came and said to them, "All authority in heaven and on earth has been given to me. Go therefore and make disciples of all nations, baptizing them in the name of the Father and of the Son and of the Holy Spirit, teaching them to observe all that I have commanded you. And behold, I am with you always, to the end of the age." *Matthew 28:1–10, 16–20*

Concise Commentary

When the angel of the Lord appeared to "Mary Magdalene and the other Mary" (Matt. 28:1) at the tomb, he told them to tell the other disciples some important information. First, Jesus "is risen from the dead" (28:7); second, they were to journey to Galilee, the place where Jesus first called them and would soon appear to them. When the disciples arrived in Galilee, sure enough Jesus showed up, and "when they saw him they worshiped him" (28:17). They worshiped him because he had proven by his resurrection that he was truly God in the flesh. We should worship him too! Then Jesus gave them the Great

Commission, important instructions regarding their important mission. But before he spoke of what they should do he said something important about who he is. He said, "All authority in heaven and on earth has been given to me" (28:17). We worship a risen King who has all authority over everything!

After our powerful risen King said that about himself, he said this to his earliest disciples: "Go therefore, and make disciples of all nations" (28:19). Just like Jesus made disciples, his disciples are to make disciples. *Of whom?* The nations; that is, people from every country, every group, and every language throughout the world. *How are we to make disciples?* By "teaching them" what Jesus taught and "baptizing them in the name of the Father and of the Son and of the Holy Spirit" (28:19, 20). *How are we to accomplish this great task?* Through Jesus's presence: "And behold, I am with you always" and for all time (28:20). Jesus's Great Commission continues to be his church's mission: his church is to go tell all people the good news that Jesus taught and to baptize them in the name of the Father, the Son, and the Holy Spirit.

Prayer Prompt
Take time to ask God, through his Spirit, to renew your vision for local evangelism and global missions. And, as he taught his disciples to "pray earnestly to the Lord of the harvest to send out laborers into his harvest" (Matt. 9:38), pray now that God would equip and encourage you and others to share your faith today with someone and to pray, even now and specifically, for the lost people that God has put in your life—at home, at work, in your extended family, and around the neighborhood.

Memory Verse
And Jesus came and said to them, "All authority in heaven and on earth has been given to me. Go therefore and make disciples of all nations, baptizing them in the name of the Father and of the Son

and of the Holy Spirit, teaching them to observe all that I have commanded you. And behold, I am with you always, to the end of the age." *Matthew 28:18–20*

• • •

"O for a Thousand Tongues to Sing"
Charles Wesley • *1739*

O for a thousand tongues to sing
my great Redeemer's praise,
the glories of my God and King,
the triumphs of his grace!

My gracious Master and my God,
assist me to proclaim,
to spread thro' all the earth abroad
the honors of thy name.

Jesus! the name that charms our fears,
that bids our sorrows cease,
'tis music in the sinner's ears,
'tis life and health and peace.

He breaks the power of cancelled sin,
he sets the prisoner free;
his blood can make the foulest clean;
his blood availed for me.

Witness

Part 4 of 5

Adoration
Pray the prayer below. Then pause to praise God for who he is and what he has done.

I will proclaim the name of the Lord and ascribe greatness to you, my God, for you are a great Lord and greatly to be praised. I will praise you, O Lord, among the nations, and sing praises to your name. I will tell of all your wondrous works! I will tell of your salvation from day to day and declare your glory among the nations, your marvelous works among all the peoples.   *Based on Deuteronomy 32:3; 2 Samuel 22:50; 1 Chronicles 16:9, 23–25*

Confession
Pray the prayer below. Then take time to ask God through Jesus to forgive specific sins.

My God, I am sorry for my sins. In choosing to do wrong and failing to do good I have sinned against you, whom I should love above all things. Please forgive me. Fill me with the Holy Spirit, that I might live a life pleasing to you. Help me to abide in Christ, that I might bear fruit. In Jesus's name, my God, have mercy. Amen.   *Act of Contrition*

Thanksgiving

Thank God for the truth that "If we confess our sins, he is faithful and just to forgive us our sins and to cleanse us from all unrighteousness" (1 John 1:9), then pray the prayer below. Finally, take time to thank God for specific blessings in your life. Also feel free to offer Psalm 118:1 ("Oh give thanks to the LORD, for he is good; for his steadfast love endures forever!") as a repeated refrain as you list off (and lift up!) to God people, events, gifts, and circumstances for which you are thankful.

Oh give thanks to the LORD; call upon his name;
    make known his deeds among the peoples!
Sing to him, sing praises to him;
    tell of all his wondrous works!   Psalm 105:1–2

Supplication

After you pray the prayer below, feel free to add your own specific requests.

May I, while I pass through this world of sense, walk by faith and not by sight, and be strong in faith, giving glory to God. May your grace, O Lord, which has appeared to all men, and appeared to me, with such glorious evidence and luster, effectually teach me to deny ungodliness and worldly lusts, and to live soberly, righteously, and godly! Work in my heart that godliness, which is profitable unto all things. Teach me, by the influence of your blessed Sprit, to love you, the Lord my God, with all my heart, and with all my soul, and with all my mind, and with all my strength. Amen.   Philip Doddridge

Prayer of Illumination

"The grass withers, the flower fades, but the word of our God will stand forever" (Isa. 40:8). Eternal God, illuminate my mind with the enduring light of your eternal word so as to guide and sustain me throughout my fleeting life. Amen.

• • •

Scripture Reading

But Saul, still breathing threats and murder against the disciples of the Lord, went to the high priest and asked him for letters to the synagogues at Damascus, so that if he found any belonging to the Way, men or women, he might bring them bound to Jerusalem. Now as he went on his way, he approached Damascus, and suddenly a light from heaven shone around him. And falling to the ground, he heard a voice saying to him, "Saul, Saul, why are you persecuting me?" And he said, "Who are you, Lord?" And he said, "I am Jesus, whom you are persecuting. But rise and enter the city, and you will be told what you are to do." The men who were traveling with him stood speechless, hearing the voice but seeing no one. Saul rose from the ground, and although his eyes were opened, he saw nothing. So they led him by the hand and brought him into Damascus. And for three days he was without sight, and neither ate nor drank.

Now there was a disciple at Damascus named Ananias. The Lord said to him in a vision, "Ananias." And he said, "Here I am, Lord." And the Lord said to him, "Rise and go to the street called Straight, and at the house of Judas look for a man of Tarsus named Saul, for behold, he is praying, and he has seen in a vision a man named Ananias come in and lay his hands on him so that he might regain his sight." But Ananias answered, "Lord, I have heard from many about this man, how much evil he has done to your saints at Jerusalem. And here he has authority from the chief priests to bind all who call on your name." But the Lord said to him, "Go, for he is a chosen instrument of mine to carry my name before the Gentiles and kings and the children of Israel. For I will show him how much he must suffer for the sake of my name." So Ananias departed and entered the house. And laying his hands on him he said, "Brother Saul, the Lord Jesus who appeared to you on the road by which you came has sent me so that you may regain your sight and be filled with the Holy Spirit." And immediately something like scales fell from his eyes, and he regained his sight. Then he rose and was baptized; and taking food, he was strengthened.

For some days he was with the disciples at Damascus. And immediately he proclaimed Jesus in the synagogues, saying, "He is the Son of God." And all who heard him were amazed and said, "Is not this the man who made havoc in Jerusalem of those who called upon this name? And has he not come here for this purpose, to bring them bound before the chief priests?" But Saul increased all the more in strength, and confounded the Jews who lived in Damascus by proving that Jesus was the Christ.   Acts 9:1–22

Concise Commentary

Acts 9:1–2 begins with a description of a merciless murderer on a merciless mission: "But Saul, still breathing threats and murder against the disciples of the Lord, went to the high priest and asked him for letters to the synagogues at Damascus, so that if he found any belonging to the Way [Christians], men or women, he might bring them [150 miles!] bound to Jerusalem." On Saul's way to Damascus, however, Jesus had a different plan. He saved him, completely changed him, and gave him a new mission. A scene that began with Saul's seeking to kill Christians ends with Saul's (also called Paul) preaching a sermon that proclaims "[Jesus] is the Son of God" (9:20). By God's amazing grace Saul goes from persecutor to preacher. God's grace knows no limits. God can, and does, call greedy tax collectors (like Zacchaeus) and merciless murderers (like Saul). In Paul's many letters he writes about his life before and after his Damascus Road experience. Before he encountered Jesus he was "a blasphemer, persecutor, and insolent opponent" (1 Tim. 1:13), someone who intensely "persecuted the church and tried to destroy it" (Gal. 1:13). In saving Saul Jesus shows how patient and loving a Savior he is. No one is too bad to be saved. Anyone who confesses that he is sinner (however great the sins), asks for forgiveness, and believes that Jesus died for him can be saved. This is what is so great about the gospel. And is this gospel not great news that we should share with the world, even with those we think are too far from God to become Christians?

Prayer Prompt
Take time to ask God to help you believe that Jesus can save even the chief of sinners. Ask him to fill you with the Holy Spirit so you too might share with others the salvation that can be found only in Jesus Christ.

Memory Verse
And Jesus came and said to them, "All authority in heaven and on earth has been given to me. Go therefore and make disciples of all nations, baptizing them in the name of the Father and of the Son and of the Holy Spirit, teaching them to observe all that I have commanded you. And behold, I am with you always, to the end of the age." *Matthew 28:18–20*

• • •

"Stricken, Smitten, and Afflicted"
Thomas Kelly • 1804

Stricken, smitten, and afflicted,
see Him dying on the tree!
'Tis the Christ by man rejected;
yes, my soul, 'tis He, 'tis He!
'Tis the long-expected Prophet,
David's Son, yet David's Lord;

by His Son God now has spoken;
'tis the true and faithful Word.

Tell me, ye who hear Him groaning,
was there ever grief like His?
Friends thro' fear His cause disowning,
foes insulting His distress;
many hands were raised to wound Him,
none would interpose to save;
but the deepest stroke that pierced Him
was the stroke that Justice gave.

Ye who think of sin but lightly,
nor suppose the evil great,
here may view its nature rightly,
here its guilt may estimate.
Mark the sacrifice appointed;
see who bears the awful load;
'tis the Word, the Lord's Anointed,
Son of Man and Son of God.

Here we have a firm foundation,
here the refuge of the lost:
Christ the Rock of our salvation,
His the name of which we boast.
Lamb of God, for sinners wounded,
Sacrifice to cancel guilt!
None shall ever be confounded
who on Him their hope have built.

Witness

Part 5 of 5

Adoration
Pray the prayer below. Then pause to praise God for who he is and what he has done.

Oh sing to the LORD a new song;
   sing to the LORD, all the earth!
Sing to the LORD, bless his name;
   tell of his salvation from day to day.
Declare his glory among the nations,
   his marvelous works among all the peoples!   *Psalm 96:1–3*

Confession
Pray the prayer below. Then take time to ask God through Jesus to forgive specific sins.

O Father, receive again the thing that you have created. O Son, receive the thing that you have governed. O Holy Spirit, fetch the thing that you so bountifully have preserved. Three persons and one very God, I entreat you: remember not my offenses forever. For I cry, Lord God and Father, mercy. Lord God Son, mercy. Lord God Holy Spirit, mercy. Amen.
Martin Luther

Thanksgiving

Thank God for the truth that "If we confess our sins, he is faithful and just to forgive us our sins and to cleanse us from all unrighteousness" (1 John 1:9), then pray the prayer below. Finally, take time to thank God for specific blessings in your life. Also feel free to offer Psalm 118:1 ("Oh give thanks to the Lord, for he is good; for his steadfast love endures forever!") as a repeated refrain as you list off (and lift up!) to God people, events, gifts, and circumstances for which you are thankful.

My Lord Jesus, you are "the faithful witness, the firstborn from the dead, and the ruler of the kings of the earth," and I thank you today that you have loved me, freed me from my sins by your blood, and grafted me into your kingdom as a priest who loves and serves you. Amen.   *Based on Revelation 1:5*

Supplication

After you pray the prayer below, feel free to add your own specific requests.

Due to the saving mercies given to me in Jesus Christ, I present my body as a living sacrifice, holy and acceptable to you, O Lord. By the power of your Spirit help me not to be conformed to this world but to be transformed by the renewal of my mind, so I might be able to discern your will, to know what is good and acceptable and perfect in your sight. By the grace given to me, humble me. May I not think more highly of myself than I ought to think, but think with sober judgment and according to the measure of the faith bestowed upon me. May I love your people, know my own gifts, acknowledge the gifts of others, and walk alongside members of my local church so as to strengthen the body of Christ universal. Let my love for you and others to be genuine and with brotherly affection. Help me to be zealous and fervent in spirit as I serve you. Help me to rejoice in hope, be patient in tribulation, and constant in prayer. May I be generous with my money, contributing to the needs of the saints throughout the world and in my home (showing hospitality), and may I be sympathetic (rejoicing with those who rejoice and weeping with those who weep). Amen.   *A prayer based on Romans 12:1–4, 9–13, 15*

Prayer of Illumination
O Holy Spirit, as the sun is full of light, the ocean full of water, and heaven full of glory, so may my heart be full of you. Come as love, that I may adore the Father and love him as my all. Come as power, to expel every rebel lust and to reign supreme and keep me yours. Come as joy, to dwell in me, move in me, animate me. Come as sanctifier, with my body, soul, and spirit wholly yours. Come as helper, with strength to bless and keep, directing my every step. Come as beautifier, bringing order out of confusion, loveliness out of chaos. Come as light, illuminating the Scripture, molding me in its laws. Come as teacher, leading me into all truth, filling me with all understanding. Amen.   *Valley of Vision*[43]

• • •

Scripture Reading
So put away all malice and all deceit and hypocrisy and envy and all slander. Like newborn infants, long for the pure spiritual milk, that by it you may grow up into salvation—if indeed you have tasted that the Lord is good.

As you come to him, a living stone rejected by men but in the sight of God chosen and precious, you yourselves like living stones are being built up as a spiritual house, to be a holy priesthood, to offer spiritual sacrifices acceptable to God through Jesus Christ. For it stands in Scripture:

"Behold, I am laying in Zion a stone,
    a cornerstone chosen and precious,
and whoever believes in him will not be put to shame."

So the honor is for you who believe, but for those who do not believe,

> "The stone that the builders rejected
> has become the cornerstone,"

and

> "A stone of stumbling,
> and a rock of offense."

They stumble because they disobey the word, as they were destined to do.

But you are a chosen race, a royal priesthood, a holy nation, a people for his own possession, that you may proclaim the excellencies of him who called you out of darkness into his marvelous light. Once you were not a people, but now you are God's people; once you had not received mercy, but now you have received mercy.

Beloved, I urge you as sojourners and exiles to abstain from the passions of the flesh, which wage war against your soul. Keep your conduct among the Gentiles honorable, so that when they speak against you as evildoers, they may see your good deeds and glorify God on the day of visitation.   1 Peter 2:1–12

Concise Commentary

Peter crams many deep theological truths into a few verses. He also quotes multiple Old Testament texts and masterfully connects them to the work of Jesus Christ and to man's reception or rejection of Christ. More than that, he provides a clear and concise definition of Christian witness. Evangelism is *declaring and demonstrating the excellencies of Christ*. The first aspect of this definition (declaration) comes from verses 9–10. We are to "proclaim the excellencies of him [Jesus]" (2:9b). Why? Two reasons, or motivations, are given. The first has to do with our *identity*: we "are a chosen race, a royal priesthood, a holy nation, a people for his own possession" (2:9a); "once you were not a people, but now you are God's people" (2:10a); we have been shown mercy (we have been "called . . . out of darkness into his marvelous light," 2:9c; "once you had not received mercy, but now you have received mercy," 2:10b). The second motivation relates to *godly behavior* ("your good behavior in Christ," 3:16). Christians are a "holy nation" (2:9) because we have been called to be "a royal priesthood," people who "offer spiritual sacrifices acceptable to God through Jesus Christ" (2:5). Our holiness does not make us right with God, but our holy actions are pleasing and acceptable to God due to Christ's perfect righteousness on our behalf.

Moreover, our godly behavior is not only a pleasing aroma to God but an alluring one to unbelievers (3:1–2), the second aspect of our definition of evangelism (demonstration of Christ's excellencies). When we "keep [our] conduct among the Gentiles honorable" (2:12)—when we "put away all malice and all deceit and hypocrisy and envy and all slander" (2:1); "abstain from the passions of the flesh, which wage war against" our souls (2:11); and live as though this world's values are not ours and heaven is our home (we walk in this world "as sojourners and exiles," 2:11)—the unbelieving world may take notice. Peter puts it this way: "They may see your good deeds and glorify God on the day of visitation" (2:12). Jesus says it this way: "Let your light shine before others, so that they may see your good works and give glory to your Father who is in heaven" (Matt. 5:16). Both sayings speak of mankind's coming to know Christ and thus bringing glory to God.

Prayer Prompt
Take time to ask God, through his Spirit, to remind you that "you are the light of the world" and, as light in this dark world, to put your light "on a stand" so it might give "light to all"

around you (Matt. 5:14, 15). Also pray that you would walk in a manner worthy of the gospel—in holiness—so people might be drawn to the gospel.

Memory Verse

And Jesus came and said to them, "All authority in heaven and on earth has been given to me. Go therefore and make disciples of all nations, baptizing them in the name of the Father and of the Son and of the Holy Spirit, teaching them to observe all that I have commanded you. And behold, I am with you always, to the end of the age." *Matthew 28:18–20*

• • •

"May the Mind of Christ, My Savior"
Kate B. Wilkinson • *1925*

May the mind of Christ, my Savior,
live in me from day to day,
by His love and pow'r controlling
all I do and say.

May the word of God dwell richly
in my heart from hour to hour,
so that all may see I triumph
only through His pow'r.

May the peace of God my Father
rule my life in everything,
that I may be calm to comfort
sick and sorrowing.

May the love of Jesus fill me
as the waters fill the sea;
Him exalting, self abasing:
this is victory.

May I run the race before me,
strong and brave to face the foe,
looking only unto Jesus
as I onward go.

May His beauty rest upon me
as I seek the lost to win,
and may they forget the channel,
seeing only Him.

Notes

1. Various sentences taken from Douglas Sean O'Donnell, *Matthew: All Authority in Heaven and on Earth*, Preaching the Word (Wheaton, IL: Crossway, 2013), 764, 770; Douglas Sean O'Donnell, *Mark: Arise and Follow the Son*, vol. 3 of Expository Reflections on the Gospels (Wheaton, IL: Crossway, 2024), 419–28.

2. Adapted from Douglas Sean O'Donnell, *God's Lyrics: Rediscovering Worship through Old Testament Songs* (Phillipsburg, NJ: P&R, 2010), 90–91, 103–4. Used by Permission. The Bach illustration comes from Andrew Wilson-Dickson, *The Story of Christian Music* (Minneapolis: Fortress, 1992), 96.

3. Arthur Bennett, ed., *The Valley of Vision: A Collection of Puritan Prayers and Devotions* (1975; repr., Edinburgh: Banner of Truth Trust, 2006), 100.

4. *Valley of Vision*, 136–37.

5. Adapted from O'Donnell, *Mark*, 373–82.

6. Adapted from Douglas Sean O'Donnell, *1–3 John: A Gospel-Transformed Life*, Reformed Expository Commentary (Phillipsburg, NJ: P&R, 2015), chapter 11. Used by permission.

7. Adapted from Emily Blick and John D. Witvliet, *Worship Sourcebook*, 2nd ed. (Grand Rapids, MI: Baker, 2013), 510. Used by permission of Faith Alive Christian Resources.

8. For an excellent new song on this text and theme see Hal H. Hopson, "The Gift of Love" (1972).

9. The second half of this Concise Commentary is adapted from O'Donnell, *Matthew*, 665.

10. Based, in small part, and adapted from *Valley of Vision*, 300–301.

11. George Frideric Handel, "I Know That My Redeemer Liveth," *Messiah*, 1741.

12. Adapted, in part, from Douglas Sean O'Donnell, *Job*, in *Ezra–Job*, vol. 4 of ESV Expository Commentary (Wheaton, IL: Crossway, 2020), 409–13; O'Donnell, *Job: Where Wisdom Is Found*, Reformed Expository Commentary (Phillipsburg, NJ: P&R, forthcoming). Used by permission.

13. Adapted from Blick and Witvliet, *Worship Sourcebook*, 411. Used by permission of Faith Alive Christian Resources.
14. Douglas Sean O'Donnell, *The Beginning and End of Wisdom: Preaching Christ from the First and Last Chapters of Proverbs, Ecclesiastes, and Job* (Wheaton, IL: Crossway, 2011), 45.
15. See O'Donnell, *Beginning and End of Wisdom*, 35–37.
16. Adapted from O'Donnell, *Job*, in *Ezra–Job*, 453–598; O'Donnell, *Job: Where Wisdom Is Found*. Used by permission.
17. *Valley of Vision*, xxiv–xxv.
18. Adapted from O'Donnell, *Beginning and End of Wisdom*, 29; O'Donnell, *Job: Where Wisdom Is Found*. Used by permission.
19. For a new tune ("Gunnar") and arrangement see Edwin T. Childs, b. 1945, Tune © Copyright 1999 by MorningStar Music Publishers.
20. Adapted from *Valley of Vision*, 98–99.
21. As connected in Ryan Kelly, *Calls to Worship, Invocations, and Benedictions* (Phillipsburg, NJ: P&R, 2022), 83.
22. Adapted from *Valley of Vision*, 134.
23. Adapted slightly from J. I. Packer's opening prayer at one of the meetings of the Translation Oversight Committee of the ESV.
24. Adapted from *Valley of Vision*, 214.
25. Adapted, in part, from O'Donnell, *God's Lyrics*, chapter 4. Used by permission.
26. Adapted from, and added to, Barbara R. Duguid, *Streams of Mercy: Prayers of Confession and Celebration*, ed. Iain M. Duguid (Phillipsburg, NJ: P&R, 2018), 20–21. Used by permission.
27. Adapted from Duguid, *Streams of Mercy*, 48–49. Used by permission.
28. Adapted from O'Donnell, *1–3 John*, 17–20. Used by permission.
29. Adapted from the prayer of confession, compiled by Brian Martin, Christ Presbyterian Church (Wheaton, IL), October 29, 2023. Based on lines from the Beatitudes; James 3:13–18; and language borrowed from the Book of Common Prayer and Barbara R. Duguid, *Prone to Wander: Prayers of Confession and Celebration*, ed. Iain M. Duguid (Phillipsburg, NJ: P&R, 2014), 94. Used by permission.
30. Adapted from *Valley of Vision*, 78–79.
31. Adapted, in part, from O'Donnell, *Mark*, 234–35.
32. Adapted from Duguid, *Streams of Mercy*, 48–49. Used by permission.
33. Adapted, in part, from O'Donnell, *Mark*, 474–78; O'Donnell, *Matthew*, 786.
34. Adapted from *Valley of Vision*, 210.
35. Adapted from *Daily Prayer*, ed. Eric Milner-White and G. W. Briggs (Harmondsworth, UK: Penguin, 1959), http.//assets.newscriptorium.com /collects-and-prayers/daily_prayer.htm; building on the words of John

Donne, sermon 146, on Acts 7:60, preached at Whitehall, February 29, 1627. Quoted in David Gibson, *The Lord of Psalm 23: Jesus Our Shepherd, Companion, and Host* (Wheaton, IL: Crossway, 2023), 143–44.

36. Alec Motyer, *New Bible Commentary* (Leicester, UK: Inter-Varsity, 1994), 500.

37. See Gibson, *Lord of Psalm 23*, 5, 16.

38. Gibson, *Lord of Psalm 23*, 19 (see also p. 4).

39. "In the Hebrew of Psalm 23 there are twenty lines (including the title), and line ten—the exact midpoint of the psalm—is this 'for you are with me.'" Gibson, *Lord of Psalm 23*, 57.

40. For two other excellent songs on Psalm 23 see "The Lord's My Shepherd, I'll Want Not" from the 1650 Scottish Psalter (set to "Crimond" or "Wilshire") and Christopher Idle, "The Lord My Shepherd Rules My Life" (1977), set to the tune "St Columba."

41. Adapted from *Valley of Vision*, 282–83.

42. For a new tune and arrangement see Kevin Twit, "I Heard the Voice of Jesus Say" ©1998 Kevin Twit Music.

43. Reordered and adapted from *Valley of Vision*, 50–51.

For Further Reading

Allen, Richard. *The Life, Experience, and Gospel Labours of the Rt. Rev. Richard Allen. To which Is Annexed the Rise and Progress of the African Methodist Episcopal Church in the United States of America. Containing a Narrative of the Yellow Fever in the Year of Our Lord 1793: With an Address to the People of Colour in the United States*. 1833.

Basil: Letters and Select Works. Edited by By Philip Schaff and Henry Wace. Nicene and Post-Nicene Fathers 2.8. New York: The Christian Literature Co., 1985.

Baxter, Richard. *The Practical Works of the Late Reverend and Pious Richard Baxter*. London: Thomas Parkhurst, 1707.

Bayly, Lewis. *The Practice of Piety: A Puritan Devotional Manual*. Grand Rapids, MI: Soli Deo Gloria Publications, 2019.

Bennett, Arthur, ed. *The Valley of Vision: A Collection of Puritan Prayers and Devotions*. Edinburgh: Banner of Truth Trust, 2006.

Bevins, Winfield. *Our Common Prayer: A Field Guide to the Book of Common Prayer*. Simeon Press, 2013.

Brooks, Thomas. *The Mute Christian under the Smart Rod; with Sovereign Antidotes for Every Case*. 48th ed. London: W. Nicholson, 1806.

Burgess, Anthony. *The True Doctrine of Justification: Asserted, and Vindicated, from the Errors of Papists, Arminians, Socinians, and More Especially Antinomians*. London: Robert White, 1648.

Calvin, John. *Institutes of the Christian Religion*. Library of Christian Classics. Edited by John T. McNeill. Translated by Ford Lewis Battles. Philadelphia: Westminster, 1960.

Chester, Tim. *Into His Presence: Praying with the Puritans*. Charlotte, NC: The Good Book Company, 2022.

Clarkson, David. *The Works of David Clarkson*. Edinburgh: John Greig and Son, Old Physic Gardens. 1864–1865.

Collins, Owen, ed. *Classic Christian Prayers: A Celebration of Praise and Glory*. New York: Testament Books, 1999.

Common Prayer: Resources for Gospel-Shaped Gatherings. Sydney: Anglican Press Australia, 2012.

Cyril of Jerusalem. "Catechetical Lecture 17." In *Cyril of Jerusalem, Gregory of Nazianzen*. Edited by Philip Schaff and Henry Wace. Nicene and Post-Nicene Father 2.7. New York: The Christian Literature Co., 1894.

Doddridge, Philip. *The Works of Rev. P. Doddridge, D.D. in Ten Volumes*. Leeds, UK: Edward Raines, 1802.

Edwards, Jonathan. *The Works of Jonathan Edwards*. Edited by Edward Hickman. 2 vols. Reprint. Carlisle, PA: Banner of Truth, 1992. 1:680–682.

Elmer, Robert, ed. *Fount of Heaven: Prayers of the Early Church*. Bellingham, WA: Lexham, 2022.

———. *Piercing Heaven: Prayers of the Puritans*. Bellingham, WA: Lexham, 2019.

Gibson, Jonathan. *Be Thou My Vision: A Liturgy for Daily Worship*. Wheaton, IL: Crossway, 2021.

———. *O Come, O Come, Emmanuel: A Liturgy for Daily Worship from Advent to Epiphany*. Wheaton, IL: Crossway, 2023.

Griffith, Bobby G., Jr. *Confessions of Sin and Assurance of Pardon—A Pocket Resource*. Ross-shire, UK: Christian Focus, 2016.

Henry, Matthew. *A Method for Prayer: With Scripture Expressions, Proper to Be Used under Each Head; With Directions for Daily Communion with God, Showing How to Begin, How to Spend, and How to Close Every Day with God*. Glasgow: D. Mackenzie, 1834.

Hughes, R. Kent, and Douglas Sean O'Donnell. *The Pastor's Book: A Comprehensive and Practical Guide to Pastoral Ministry*. Wheaton, IL: Crossway, 2015.

Johnson, Terry L. *Leading in Worship: A Sourcebook for Presbyterian Students and Ministers Drawing From the Biblical and Historical Forms of the Reformed Tradition.* Revised edition. Powder Springs, GA: Tolle Lege Press, 2013.

Plummer, Charles, ed. *Devotions from Ancient and Medieval Sources (Western).* 1916.

Reynolds, Edward. *The Whole Works of the Right Rev. Edward Reynolds D. D.* London, 1826.

Scholasticus, Serapion. *Bishop Serapion's Prayer-Book: An Egyptian Pontifical Dated Probably about A.D. 350–56.* Edited by John Wordsworth. Translated by G. Wobbermin. London: SPCK, 1899.

Stewart, Dorothy M., ed. *The Westminster Collection of Prayers.* Louisville: Westminster John Knox, 2021.

Stewart, Maria W. "A Prayer for Purification (1835)." In *Meditations from the Pen of Mrs. Maria W. Stewart.* 1879.

Tercentenary Monument: In Commemoration of the Three Hundredth Anniversary of the Heidelberg Catechism. M. Kieffer & Company, 1863.

The Book of Common Worship. Philadelphia, 1906.

Thomas à Kempis. *The Imitation of Christ.* Translated by John Payne. Glasgow: William Collins, 1839.

Thornton, Henry. *Devotional Prayers.* Chicago: Moody, 1993.

———. *Family Prayers and Prayers on the Ten Commandments.* London: Standford and Swords, 1834.

Torrance, Thomas F. *Christian Doctrine of God: One Being Three Persons.* London: A&C Black, 2001.

Washington, James Melvin, ed. *Conversations with God: Two Centuries of Prayers by African Americans.* New York: HarperColllins, 1994.

Wax, Trevin K. *Psalms in 30 Days.* Nashville: Holman, 2021.

Wheatley, Phillis. "Prayer of Phillis's Accidentally Discovered in Her Bible," 30 June 1779, microfilm. Schomburg Center for Research in Black Culture, New York Public Library. Included in *Complete Writings.* Edited by Vincent Carretta. New York: Penguin, 2001.